The 25
Biblical Laws
of Partnership
with God

The 25 Biblical Laws *of* Partnership with God

POWERFUL PRINCIPLES *for* SUCCESS

IN LIFE *and* WORK

WILLIAM DOUGLAS

AND RUBENS TEIXEIRA

BakerBooks

a division of Baker Publishing Group
Grand Rapids, Michigan

© 2020 by William Douglas and Rubens Teixeira

Published by Baker Books
a division of Baker Publishing Group
PO Box 6287, Grand Rapids, MI 49516-6287
www.bakerbooks.com

Printed in the United States of America

Library of Congress Cataloging-in-Publication Data
Names: Douglas, William, 1967– author. | Teixeira, Rubens, 1970– author.
Title: The 25 biblical laws of partnership with God : powerful principles for success in life and work / William Douglas and Rubens Teixeira.
Other titles: The twenty-five biblical laws of partnership with God
Description: Grand Rapids, Michigan : Baker Books, a division of Baker Publishing Group, 2020. | Includes bibliographical references.
Identifiers: LCCN 2019041772 | ISBN 9780801094828 (paperback)
Subjects: LCSH: Success—Religious aspects—Christianity. | Success—Biblical teaching. | Success in business.
Classification: LCC BV4598.3 .D679 2020 | DDC 248.4—dc23
LC record available at https://lccn.loc.gov/2019041772

20 21 22 23 24 25 26   7 6 5 4 3 2 1

For Nayara, Luísa, Lucas, and Samuel

William Douglas

For my wife, Marta;
my children, Renan and Mateus;
my parents, Paulo and Darcy;
and my brother, Paulo Teixeira

Rubens Teixeira

You are in error because you do
not know the Scriptures or the
power of God.

Matthew 22:29

Those who trust in the LORD will
prosper.

Proverbs 28:25

CONTENTS

7

INTRODUCTION

What Is Partnership with God?

The highest heavens belong to the LORD, but the
earth He has given to mankind.

Psalm 115:16 *

Who wouldn't want to have Warren Buffett, Bill Gates, or
Jorge Paulo Lemann as a business partner? Who wouldn't
want to own a stake, however small, in one of their spectacu-
lar companies? It is inspiring to be around innovative people
and ventures. Sometimes the most important thing is not the
size of the business but its vision and mission.

If you think these examples are enticing, how would you
react to the opportunity to become a partner with God? Have
you ever imagined what it would be like to be a part of His
projects or to be able to count on Him to develop your own?

If you think partnership with God would be amazing, then this book may change your life.

God as Your Business Partner

In the world of business, it isn't easy to form a partnership with a successful business executive. You must bring a lot to offer your potential partner, such as capital or talent. To be God's partner, you might assume that you would need to meet extremely high standards. Not so. God is willing to associate with those who don't seem to have anything to offer and even with those who have a disreputable background but desire to change. God values and invests in people. His projects are focused on people, not on real estate, products, or money. The most important thing to God is a person's commitment to God's vision, mission, and values.

The Bible affirms God's interest in walking alongside us and participating in our daily activities, whether they involve business matters or personal issues related to family or health. Some people, like the biblical character Jabez, simply ask God for help; they want God to support them without offering Him anything in return (1 Chron. 4:9–10). Others show gratitude to God, like Jacob who promised to give back a tenth of all that God gave him (Gen. 28:20–22).

Then there are those who ask God for nothing and offer Him 100 percent of all they have, such as the apostle Peter, a fisherman who "left everything" to follow Jesus (Mark 10:28). In short, we all have the opportunity to associate with God in all areas of our lives.

Handing over your decisions and your convictions to God—in full or in part—takes a lot of <u>faith</u>. <u>Faith</u> is the <u>belief</u> ~~that~~ God will act, at the appropriate <u>time</u>, moved by immense <u>wisdom</u>, goodness, and sovereignty. You must have <u>faith</u> to pray, to remain in an unpleasant place, and to <u>believe</u> ~~that~~ God will change your situation at the <u>opportune</u> <u>time</u>, ⚡ according to His plans.

Whether your <u>focus</u> is your career, your finances, or a business you are starting or managing, when you are in partnership with God, each party has rights and responsibilities, burdens and rewards. God, in this respect, is similar to any partner: He will contribute with His "capital" and with His "work," and He expects ~~that~~ you will do your part to make the project take off and pay dividends for both of you.

God as Your Adviser and Coach

God can be regarded not only as a partner or a powerful investor but also as a mentor, coach, and adviser in order to <u>create</u> a solid foundation for your life project.

Consider the example of Zacchaeus, a tax collector (Luke 19:1–10). After having lunch with Jesus, Zacchaeus decided to give up his corrupt ways, return the money he had cheated from taxpayers, and share his fortune with the poor. Jesus exercised a strong influence over His new partner, resulting in a change in the way Zacchaeus managed his career and finances.

You may be asking yourself, *As a flawed person, what do I have to offer God? What results can He expect from our partnership?* First, God wants to see His partner—you—happy. Second, He wants to use your job, your career, and your business (whether you are the owner or an employee) for His divine purposes. God desires to be your partner and to bless your plans, but He expects you to follow some guide-lines, which we will discover in this book.

God's expectations are similar to what a board of directors or a real-life business partner would ask of you. We are talking about mission, vision, and values; about how to recruit, maintain, and reward your shareholders and coworkers; about incentive policies and distribution of dividends.

If you have already dedicated your life to God, then strengthening your partnership with Him should be a natural next step. But even if you aren't religious or have distanced yourself from religion, this is not a reason to keep you from benefiting from God's advice for successful and ethical business practices.

The idea of a partnership with God might seem bold, pretentious, or even shocking, but what if the Bible is about a living God who desires to have a relationship with us—a God who really does want to go to work with us? From what we read in the Scriptures, God wants to be a part of every aspect of our lives, not just the spiritual part. He wants to participate in our personal lives, our family lives, our careers, our workplaces, and in the ways we do business.

If God wanted to be your partner, would you at least set up a meeting with Him to discuss the proposal? Would you be interested in reading the prospectus or the brochure in which the eternal investor outlines His plans and His methodology?

What Are the Spiritual Laws?

If you want to know what a proposal for partnership with God would look like, rest assured ~~that~~ it is already on the table; it was written centuries ago. It is in the Bible and can be expressed in some spiritual laws that will be addressed in this book. Spiritual laws are a part of the laws of nature and, though immaterial, they are as unwavering and as powerful as laws of physics. There is no way to escape their consequences, just as there is no way to escape the law of gravity or the law of magnetism.

In our previous book, *The 25 Biblical Laws of Success*, we dealt with this cause-and-effect relationship and concentrated on twenty-five spiritual laws that apply to everyone, regardless of whether you are religious or <u>believe</u> in God. In this book, we will address twenty-five different spiritual laws ~~that are~~ directed at those who have <u>faith</u> in God and desire a higher standard of success and excellence. The laws of partnership with God, which are deeper and more comprehensive than the laws of success, are more effective with regard not only to business but also to quality of life and the search for a deeper meaning behind our existence.

In this book, we deal with leadership and teamwork, as well as personal ethics and service to others. Furthermore, we discuss the power of prayer and the miracles that can occur in a career, in business, and in finances. We wrote this book for those who <u>believe</u> ~~that~~ professional success can be achieved in harmony with God's plans for our lives. As we will see, the Bible offers us reliable guidelines and remarkable results.

In essence, we will analyze the deeper spiritual laws that apply to those who <u>believe</u> in God and desire to partner with Him.

Was Jesus Interested in Business and Careers?

How would you react if you heard ~~that~~ in early first-century Israel, an unusual teacher told stories in which He spoke of workers, vineyards, and cash investments? Well, it's <u>true</u>. In His stories, Jesus of Nazareth talked about dishonest administrators, creditors who didn't forgive debts (and others who did), tax collectors, valuable pearls, and hidden treasure. Work, career, and business matters were topics ~~that~~ Jesus frequently addressed; in fact, He had quite a lot to say about them.

Jesus talked about these topics because people were interested in them. Aside from offering important lessons on these issues, He used everyday situations to describe the problems of the soul. The Bible seems to indicate ~~that~~ Jesus wanted to make changes not only in the way people <u>practiced</u> religion but also in how they conducted their careers and businesses. He had <u>wise</u> advice for administrators, managers, employees—even government officials!

Unfortunately, not everyone looks favorably on mixing <u>faith</u> and business. On the one hand, certain religious groups remove themselves so completely from the world that, in contrast to Jesus, they lose touch with the problems people face on a daily basis. On the other hand, some religious groups are comfortable in an unethical world because ethical precepts make it more difficult for them to exploit people.

The successful businessperson understands ~~that~~ integrity and religious values can aid the development of any activity, especially those involving balanced, harmonious, and respectful relationships among people. Christianity tends to produce sensible, hardworking people.

What is missing from the corporate world is a little more religion—or at least the values ~~that~~ religion advocates: honesty instead of cheating, integrity and solidarity instead of exploitation, social and environmental responsibility instead of greed, sustainability instead of deterioration. All these values are found in the Bible and can be applied by anyone who deems them important—Christians, Jews, Muslims, agnostics, and atheists alike.

One of the problems of Western society is ~~that~~ even though a majority of people say they believe the Bible is a sacred book (or at least a book of wisdom), Biblical values remain locked up in the church and are not applied to everyday life. While religion is indeed about an encounter of the soul with God, Biblical values need to have an impact on our daily lives.

The application of the Golden Rule—"Do to others what you would have them do to you" (Matt. 7:12)—as well as other Biblical behaviors, such as honesty and compassion, reveal ~~that~~ God's influence is present in someone's life. Of course, you do not need to be a follower of God to behave in an ethical and charitable way; indeed, there are many atheists and nonreligious people who have these qualities. What is not acceptable is when people who claim to follow the Bible do not live according to its recommendations.

The Bible is a source of eternal wisdom ~~that~~ we can apply to our professional and corporate lives. The teachings of the Bible are not just about love, solidarity, and kindness. The Bible also deals with pragmatic subjects for those who ~~wish~~ *desire* to get ahead in life, get a good job, start a business, build successful teams, train effective leaders, plan well, and invest wisely. As demonstrated through the parables Jesus told, the Bible is not afraid to mix faith and business. This is why we can use its lessons as the basis for guiding our conduct in the world of business and finance.

Servant or Partner?

The twenty-five biblical laws of partnership with God described in this book are compelling and will likely raise a series of questions in your mind: Will you feel comfortable knowing you are no longer the sole owner of your business or career because you now have a powerful partner? Will you be able to see ~~that~~ having a difficult or frustrating job could be a positive, maybe even an honorable, mission or God-given training? Will you consider praying to ask God for a miracle in your business or career? If you want to be in partnership with God, you should be prepared to work with dedication and efficiency, to seek God's wisdom and put it into practice, to treat others as you ~~wish~~ *desire* to be treated, and to work more than you are required to. By applying these Biblical principles, you will be able to obtain excellent results, as we explained in *The 25 Biblical Laws of Success*.

But anyone can follow the twenty-five biblical laws of success. In this book, the process of applying spiritual laws gets more serious. The twenty-five Biblical laws of partnership with God are not simply for the purpose of getting rich or being successful. Their main purpose is to develop the virtues of love, faith, devotion, gratitude, and other sentiments that go beyond the simple (and honorable) desire to succeed in life. As you dive into this book, you need to decide whether you want to be someone who truly serves God or someone who is merely interested in knowing what it is like to have God as a partner. In either case, you will need to know how to put these spiritual laws into practice in order to reap the dividends of this partnership.

While this new set of laws can bring you practical results, credibility, and respect, ideally you will follow these Biblical teachings out of love and obedience to God in order to walk more closely with Him. More than being God's business partner, you should consider being His partner in life's great journey. A partnership with God goes beyond your immediate economic or professional interests. In order to sign this contract, you need to develop your faith, care about your neighbors, give up some things, and learn what requirements and conditions this all-powerful Investor asks of you.

Anyone who wants to have a partnership with God needs to adopt Biblical standards in the workplace, in business dealings, and at home. In other words, you need to use them in dealing with not only your partner in heaven but also your partners on earth—bosses, employees, coworkers, and even your competitors, as well as family, neighbors, and friends.

A partnership with God involves a spiritual agenda with practical results. The supernatural is not inert. We should not work seeking only profit, credibility, or affection. The idea is to serve and do good works because Jesus served, did good works, and told us to imitate Him (Eph. 5:1). In short, the bylaws of this partnership entail loving God and your neighbor as yourself.

How should a Christian act at work? If the owner of a company is a follower of the Bible, how should he treat his employees and clients? Should the products sold or the services rendered by a partner of God be special in any way? Jesus told us to be different from the world, to do things differently, and to make a difference in the world for God. Working well is definitely a religious duty.

The Clauses of a Partnership with God

When God comes into your life, career, or business, it leads to a real revolution, with extraordinary possibilities, as we will see. But, before that, you need to read the contract and decide if you want to join this partnership with God. Following is a summary of the main clauses that will be analyzed in depth in this book:

- *Acknowledge God's interest in the partnership.* God is interested in being your partner in all your ventures, commercial or otherwise. It's your choice.

- *Be willing to try.* This partnership can work to a greater or lesser extent. God could be just a reference for your actions—and that would be great. Or He could become a majority stakeholder of your life. It won't hurt you to try a partnership with God in your business. Then, if you are comfortable with this model, you can adopt it for good. If God is already part of your life, you can fearlessly allow Him to take control and see the results. The good news is that God's plans are good: "'I know the plans I have for you,' declares the LORD, 'plans to prosper you and not to harm you, plans to give you hope and a future'" (Jer. 29:11).

- *Decide to think and act in extraordinary ways.* Usually, we just take care of our own interests, and we think only about material and immediate things. But dare to engage the supernatural. We suggest that you be open to the spiritual dimension of your business and career.

- *Seek ways to help others.* We are not suggesting that you must turn yourself into a martyr, a Saint Francis of Assisi, or a Gandhi. But do what you can. And then you will become an instrument of the actions of God, working as His partner in the great investment in human life. This will produce amazing results for you and those who are close to you.

Being God's partner will be good for you, your business, and your career, as well as those with whom you come into contact. As a result, you might start seeing God work directly in your life, as we have. God is looking for partners to execute His plans and dreams on earth. You can be one of them.

You, God's Partner

The first condition for becoming God's partner is to believe that He exists. Second, believe that He is interested in you. Finally, establish a relationship with Him. You might have doubts about the way God acts, and you might not be sure that He truly is concerned about your professional and financial life, but, as we have said before, it can't hurt to try. Give it a real shot and see what happens.

Even if you don't have faith in God, you can still benefit from this book's teachings. But for those who do, faith is more than believing; it's taking on a suggested behavior.

Consider the case of the apostle Peter. The Bible says that Jesus looked for Peter (then known as Simon) while He was working as a fisherman. Peter knew that on that day the sea wasn't good for fishing, but when Jesus said to throw out his nets again, he did what he was told to do: "Master, we have worked all night long but have caught nothing. Yet if you say so, I will let down the nets" (Luke 5:5 NRSV). When he chose to obey Jesus's command regarding his work, Peter caught so many fish that the nets began to tear. Though he did not believe he would catch fish, Peter did what he was told to do. That too is faith.

If you already dedicate a bit of your time to God and offer Him a part of your assets (through tithes or other contributions), if you read the Bible or claim to be a Christian, we hope you will take a bold step of faith and climb one step further in your spiritual life: try giving God more "shares" in your company.

The term *shares* is well suited because in addition to referring to the parts that divide the capital of a corporation, it's also a reminder that faith is, above all, sharing your life with ← God through your actions. Act in accordance with what the Bible recommends, and you will see results. More than believers, we are witnesses of God's actions when we allow Him to be a part of our lives and to become a partner in our projects.

If you go into partnership with God, you will experience His intervention in your professional and financial life, not only through objective principles and spiritual laws but also through His direct participation in the issues that concern you. You will notice that God intervenes in a general and constant way through the laws of nature that He created. At times, He acts in specific ways, focusing on people who need a certain action, who ask for His help, or who somehow deserve it. We will seek to show that God appears to act more often in specific situations and to help you see which ones they usually are.

Theology is very useful in the sense that it explains how God intervenes in our lives by *providence* and by *concurrence*. In the first sense, God provides what we need, such as the breath of life, health, and ideal conditions for a habitable planet. In the second sense, we are invited to participate with God—and that is where the idea of a partnership with God begins.

21

� God provides, but He also proposes ~~that~~ we do our part. In this partnership, each partner has their own duties and tasks, without taking responsibility for the other's area. Though we might like God to take care of everything, He will not honor a laid-back attitude. We shouldn't sit around waiting for what we want to fall from the sky. Nor should we assume ~~that~~ God doesn't care or won't act in our favor. We need to develop a balanced view.

In this book, we will discuss building a partnership with God, changes you can make in yourself, the laws ~~that~~ you should follow to reap the benefits of this partnership, and what you can do to improve your relationship with other partners of God. We will talk about God's typical miracles and how you can help to bring them about by your actions and attitudes.

Miracles in general depend on a partnership with God, on a combination of His will and human action. Our research and experiences confirm ~~that~~ God reveals Himself to those who seek Him. He intervenes in a special way in the lives of those who pray and who work for what they desire ~~wish~~.

Sometimes God does something supernatural, and at other times He gives you the strength to fight for what you want, as we see in this passage of the Old Testament: "You may say to yourself, 'My power and the strength of my hands have produced this wealth for me.' But remember the LORD your God, for it is He who gives you the ability to produce wealth, and so confirms His covenant, which He swore to your ancestors, as it is today" (Deut. 8:17–18).

The Bible, which is available to everyone, is an ordinary, general channel for divine intervention. Some people will follow its principles; others will not. One thing is certain: we reap the attitudes and behaviors ~~that~~ we have adopted. (This is the Law of Sowing, described in *The 25 Biblical Laws of Success.*)

Awhile ago, we received a video that had circulated on the internet showing a barber arguing with his customer, who read the Bible, about the existence of God. The barber said he didn't <u>believe</u> in God because, if He existed, there wouldn't be so much pain and suffering in the world. The customer left the shop in deep thought and bumped into a long-haired street musician with an unkempt beard. He took the musician into the barbershop and said, "See? Barbers don't exist." The barber was outraged: "What do you mean? The problem is ~~that~~ he didn't come to see me." Then the man said: "God exists. People just aren't going to Him. That is why there is so much misery in the world."[1]

If you want God to help you in your professional and financial life, then go to Him. Start with the simplest thing: read the Bible. Then apply Biblical values to your work relationships. By doing so, you will become a miracle (someone who <u>truly</u> cares about others), and you will produce miracles (the changes ~~that~~ your new attitude will generate). Take note: so-called divine intervention does not always mean ~~that~~ God opens up the heavens and pours blessings and rewards down on you; <u>sometimes</u> divine intervention involves God using you to produce blessings in the lives of others. Your partner, God, wants you to help others, whether it is your boss, your employees, your work colleagues, or your clients.

The twenty-five biblical laws of success described in our previous book are principles from Scripture that can bring positive results for anyone, regardless of whether you are religious or a practicing Christian. However, if you want to go a step further and become a partner with God, then read this book and apply the twenty-five biblical laws of partnership with God—which require a greater commitment to Biblical values and to your neighbors—to your life. Try, for example, working not out of pride but instead to make the world a better place. This will result in a leap when it comes to quality and excellence in your life. The most daring can go even further, granting God full equity control of the most important company of all—you.

There are no paths, but feet in the grass will create them.
FERREIRA GULLAR

PART I

Laws *concerning* Faith

ONE

The Law of Faith

Faith is the assurance of things hoped for, the
conviction of things not seen.

Hebrews 11:1 NASB

The first step for establishing a partnership with God is to believe that God exists and that He is willing to develop common projects with us. This is faith. As the Bible says, "Anyone who comes to [God] must believe that He exists and that He rewards those who earnestly seek Him" (Heb. 11:6).

Many people say, "I would like to have faith." Others agonize over their doubts, feel divided about the existence and the acts of God, or are troubled by the way the Bible handles certain issues.

It is part of the nature of faith to deal with doubts. Furthermore, in any relationship or partnership, there are issues that need to be straightened out. If you reflect on spiritual matters, read about the subject (as you are doing now), and are willing to apply Biblical principles, then you already have enough faith to start—or continue—the lifetime journey of knowing God.

Faith is, first of all, action. All the examples we will consider in this book have a common point: the people involved acted out of trust and, by doing so, reaped good results. What we propose in this book is for you to do the same: behave as the twenty-five biblical laws of partnership with God suggest, and watch for the results.

In the Old Testament book of Exodus, we read that Moses and the people of Israel stood facing the Red Sea when Pharaoh's army overtook them. At that moment, some wanted to surrender and return to slavery; others considered killing themselves. But Moses confidently prayed for God's help. God's answer, a mixture of reprimand and instruction about how to act, couldn't have been stronger: "Why do you cry out to me? Tell the Israelites to go forward. But you lift up your staff and stretch out your hand over the sea and divide it, that the Israelites may go into the sea on dry ground" (Exod. 14:15–16 NRSV).

Praying and just standing there, waiting for God's providence, was the solution the confident Moses envisioned—but it was not the divine solution. God wanted the people to walk. More than that, He wanted them to walk toward the sea. Faith that walks sometimes achieves that which seems impossible. When Moses obeyed, he discovered the fact that the sea couldn't resist those who marched in its direction. And the Hebrews boldly walked through the middle of the sea.

In the introduction, we quoted the biblical passage in which the apostle Peter, after a night of unsuccessful fishing, followed Jesus's advice and tried again. As in Moses's case, this episode combined <u>faith</u> and action. The fishermen had spent the entire night fishing without catching any fish; therefore, going back to cast their nets again was an act of <u>faith</u>, against Peter's common sense and professional proficiency. It is important to observe t̶h̶a̶t̶ the advice Jesus gave Peter made <u>all</u> the difference when it came to action. Jesus said, "Go out where it is deeper, and let down your nets to catch some fish" (Luke 5:4 NLT). In other words, trying again shouldn't just be a mere repetition of the same act; it should be about going deeper and doing it better the next time.

In another episode recorded in the Bible, Jesus entered a village, and from a distance ten lepers cried out to Him: "'Jesus, Master, have pity on us!' When He saw them, He said, 'Go, show yourselves to the priests.' And as they went, they were cleansed. One of them, when he saw he was healed, came back, praising God in a loud voice. He threw himself at Jesus' feet and thanked Him—and he was a Samaritan. Jesus asked, 'Were not <u>all</u> ten cleansed? Where are the other nine?'" (Luke 17:12–17). As in this healing, success is usually achieved while we are walking the path. The <u>learning</u>, the experience, and the creation of a network take place while we are moving forward. This story also reveals t̶h̶a̶t̶ the Law of Gratitude (described in *The 25 Biblical Laws of Success*) is rarely practiced. Only one of the ten men returned to thank Jesus for the divine gift they received.

You don't need to be a saint to apply the Law of Faith. You just need to listen to God's instruction and be willing to walk toward the sea, to go deeper toward something you want. Faith is hearing God's command and moving forward in obedience. It doesn't matter if your objective is to change the world, to please God, or to improve your quality of life; having faith is essential for taking the first step and for experiencing the spiritual laws described in this book.

One of the cornerstones of neurolinguistics is that we need ←
to believe in order to see. In other words, we need to have faith—to put something into practice—to get answers and results. Maybe this is what Jesus calls faith the size of a mustard seed: "Truly I tell you, if you have faith as small as a mustard seed, you can say to this mountain, 'Move from here to there,' and it will move. Nothing will be impossible for you" (Matt. 17:20). Faith, no matter how small, moves mountains.

Manifestations of the Law of Faith

The Law of Faith refers not only to faith in God's existence but also to faith in what God says and what He has planned for us. Belief in God has many ramifications, among them:

- *Faith in the future*—the result of the trust that you put in God and the plans that He has for your life: "Commit to the LORD everything you do. Then he will make your plans succeed" (Prov. 16:3 NIrV).
- *Faith in ourselves*—a product of the understanding that we are born just the way God Himself chose: "It

was you who formed my inward parts; you knit me together in my mother's womb. I praise you, for I am fearfully and wonderfully made. Wonderful are your works; that I know very well" (Ps. 139:13–14 NRSV).

- *Faith in prayer*—the result of experiencing answered prayer: "You will call on me and come and pray to me, and I will listen to you" (Jer. 29:12).

Faith is not the belief that God will do what you want. It is the belief that God will do what is right.

MAX LUCADO

TWO

The Law of Prayer

The prayer of a righteous person is powerful and
effective.

James 5:16

If we must believe ~~that~~ God exists and cares about us—the
Law of Faith—in order to become God's partner, then our
next step is to try to contact Him. Prayer is talking to God.
It is the path by which we ask God for help, thank Him for
all ~~that~~ we have, and express to Him our fears, anxieties, and
hopes. When we are in partnership with God, it is important
~~that~~ we set our problems before God in prayer—and ~~that~~ we
do this consistently and daily. As the apostle Paul said, "Pray
without ceasing" (1 Thess. 5:17 NKJV).

Is it appropriate to take our habit of prayer into our professional lives? If you think career and business are personal
subjects that are irrelevant to God, you will answer no. However, if the workplace is where you spend a good part of your

life and where you have many daily interactions, you will understand that it is a wonderful field of action in which God can achieve His greatest endeavor here on earth. Therefore, the workplace is and should be a place for prayer. ✳

We see an example of this in Daniel 2, which tells the story of Nebuchadnezzar, king of Babylon, who was deeply troubled by a dream he had. He gave orders to call forth all his advisers so that they could tell him what his dream was and what it meant. He threatened that if none of the wise men were able to give a satisfactory answer, all of them would be fired. Back then, being *fired* meant their death and the destruction of their homes.

One of the king's wise men, a godly man named Daniel, wasn't present at the meeting, but he heard about the king's decision when the head of the guards came to execute him. Tactfully, Daniel asked for some time to resolve the problem and took it before God in prayer. The mystery was revealed to him in a vision, and he thanked God, saying:

> Blessed be the name of God forever and ever,
> For wisdom and might are His.
> And He changes the times and the seasons;
> He removes kings and raises up kings;
> He gives wisdom to the wise
> And knowledge to those who have understanding.
> He reveals deep and secret things;
> He knows what is in the darkness,
> And light dwells with Him.
>
> I thank You and praise You,
> O God of my fathers;

You have given me wisdom and might,
And have now made known to me what we asked of
     You,
For You have made known to us the king's demand.
     (Dan. 2:20–23 NKJV)

Daniel informed King Nebuchadnezzar that the king had dreamed about a statue with a head of gold, a chest and arms of silver, a belly and thighs of bronze, legs of iron, and feet partly of iron and partly of clay. In the dream, the image was destroyed by a stone the size of the earth. According to Daniel's interpretation, the parts of the statue are different empires that are successively in control and in domination over the world, until one day when "the God of heaven will set up a kingdom that will never be destroyed" (Dan. 2:44).

A careful look at this episode reveals that, in some way, Daniel had already gained the confidence of the king and the head of the guards, because they both gave him time to seek a solution and listened to him more than the other advisers. But what is important to be noted here is that a work problem was taken to God in prayer, and God answered.

It is not the focus of this book to teach you how to pray or to study the subject of prayer from an academic or devotional view. What we wish to highlight is that prayer works; it changes things, and it can—or should—be practiced in the workplace to the benefit of your career or your company. Professional success is a complex subject that isn't limited to prayer, but prayer is an essential component in the fulfillment of your goals.

34

We should not overlook the fact that nearly all the divine interventions mentioned in the Bible happened after someone who had faith in God prayed and asked Him for something. The result wasn't always what the person expected, but in general an answer came from God—and extraordinary things happened.

To overcome pressure, humiliation, injustice, and other misfortunes, the apostle Paul instructed us to talk to God, because in extremely difficult situations, His help is essential. Paul wrote, "Do not be anxious about anything, but in every situation, by prayer and petition, with thanksgiving, present your requests to God" (Phil. 4:6).

If you believe in God and habitually take your requests to Him in prayer, you will benefit from a strong sense of security that will propel you on your walk with God and help you reach your goals.

Aside from being a conversation with God, prayer is a way for us to reflect on what we desire, to truly listen to ourselves, and to change ourselves. Through prayer, we can become fully aware of our mistakes and start improving our lives. Prayer not only pleases God but also helps shape those who pray.

Every time you pray, if your prayer is sincere,
there will be new feeling and new meaning in
it, which will give you fresh courage, and you
will understand that prayer is an education.

FYODOR DOSTOYEVSKY

THREE

The Law of Training

No discipline seems pleasant at the time, but
painful. Later on, however, it produces a harvest
of righteousness and peace for those who have
been trained by it.

Hebrews 12:11

When God doesn't change the circumstances, it's because He ✳
wants to change you. So instead of sitting there worrying or
whining about your situation, try to see what opportunities
are concealed behind your current situation. Take advantage
of the moment and the place in which you find yourself and
begin to serve and to learn.

Let's look at the stories of two great heroes of the Bible,
Joseph and Moses, who both went through lengthy periods
of hardship but learned how to use adversity as training for
the missions they would take on. As we will learn, the ob-

stacles we face can become our competitive advantage in the future.

Tough Training, Easy Battle

The book of Genesis recounts the story of Joseph, the son of Jacob, who suffered a harsh journey in his life but in the end became Egypt's second-in-command under Pharaoh. In Joseph's youth, he was his father's favorite child and the target of his brothers' envy. To make matters worse, he described his dreams in which even the sun, the moon, and eleven stars bowed down before him. This drove his jealous brothers to conspire against him and sell him to slave traders. Joseph was taken as a slave into the house of a rich Egyptian named Potiphar, where he worked hard and grew older.

As the Bible relates, despite his difficulties, God did not abandon Joseph: "The LORD was with Joseph, and he became a successful man; he was in the house of his Egyptian master. His master saw that the LORD was with him, and that the LORD caused all that he did to prosper in his hands. So Joseph found favor in his sight and attended him; he made him overseer of his house and put him in charge of all that he had" (Gen. 39:2–4 NRSV).

After the turn of events from favorite son to favored general manager, Joseph faced a new problem: Potiphar's wife desired to have an affair with him. Joseph rejected her proposal out of loyalty to God and to his boss. He could have taken advantage of the situation, but he preferred to act in an upright way. And what was his reward for his honesty?

Joseph was thrown into prison unjustly. What would you do if you played fairly then suffered as a result?

We believe that it doesn't pay to act dishonestly or inappropriately just because "everyone does it," or "if I don't do it, someone will," or "if I don't do it, I'll never improve my life." It is worthwhile to behave well even if at some point it causes more problems than advantages. We have witnessed over and over again that ethics and integrity will be rewarded in the end.

That is what happened with Joseph. He didn't just sit there in prison, complaining about being in a tough spot despite having adhered to the highest values. While in jail, Joseph worked hard and helped the other prisoners by interpreting their dreams without receiving any recognition or gratitude. Everything had seemed to go wrong until he was called to Pharaoh's court and received a surprise ending to his story. How did this happen?

Joseph had always been helpful and caring. Though many of the people he helped forgot about him and the promises they had made to him, Joseph didn't change his behavior. After a while, when Pharaoh needed someone who could decipher dreams, Joseph's name came to mind. Joseph was summoned to interpret Pharaoh's dream, and he correctly predicted that Egypt should prepare for a period of seven years of plenty followed by seven years of famine and shortages. Joseph was freed and became Pharaoh's right-hand man.

If you are good at what you do, one day you will be remembered—and then you will need to be ready to show your potential. Joseph's story shows that if you are doing the right

thing but still are not successful, it is because your story hasn't
ended. Have hope that in the end, those who lead upright
lives will be rewarded. The weapons used against those who
walk the right path will be used for their success, regardless
of the will of their enemies.

The process of growth and maturing is not always fast.
Much time passed from the moment Joseph was sold into
slavery to the time he was promoted by Pharaoh. And they
were not easy years, as the psalmist describes: "They bruised
his feet with shackles, his neck was put in irons" (Ps. 105:18).
The lesson we can learn from Joseph's story is that it is fu-
tile to be in a hurry; as a general rule, great success stories
develop slowly over time.

For this reason, if you are going through hardship, remember that humiliation, shame, and contempt could be the
ladder that will take you to the top. The movie *Something the
Lord Made* tells the true story of a young black man named
Vivien Thomas, who overcame difficulties and pursued his
dreams, even though they seemed impossible. At a time of op-
pressive racism in the United States, Thomas saw his chances
of studying medicine fade, but he embraced the opportunity
to work as an assistant to Dr. Alfred Blalock in his Vander-
bilt University experimental surgeries lab. Years later, their
research at the Johns Hopkins University Hospital led to
the first cardiac surgery. Even without a university diploma,
Thomas was awarded an honorary doctorate degree.[1]

As the Brazilian saying goes, "Time is lord over reason,"
and it brings rewards. If you believe in divine intervention,
then it is worth remembering what King David said: "You

prepare a table before me in the presence of my enemies. You anoint my head with oil; my cup overflows" (Ps. 23:5). This does not mean ~~that~~ you will trample your enemies but ~~that~~ they will be witnesses to your success, and you will be acknowledged for the battles you had to fight in order to finally arrive at your destination.

Joseph knew how to take advantage of all the learning opportunities he had in his life. When he was a slave in the house of a rich man, he learned how to manage large amounts of money. And note ~~that~~ being a slave did not keep him from working hard or gaining knowledge. Later, in jail, Joseph learned how to make do with very little. These experiences prepared him to manage the food supply of Egypt during the seven years of plenty as well as the seven lean years.

If you don't believe in God, notice how Joseph knew how to take advantage of everything that happened to him, turning his integrity and competence into something stronger than the crises the country faced. If you do believe in God, look at how God put his servant through a very tough version of an MBA, which yielded excellent results.

We like the military slogan "Train hard, fight easy." Do you want to succeed in tough battles? First, you need to submit to training.

Consider the statement made by Rousimar Palhares, UFC champion in Rio de Janeiro in August 2011, having beaten Dann Miller:

What makes me unique as a fighter . . . it seems I was getting prepared all the way since in Dois do Indaiá. . . . When

I first dropped school and started working in the fields, I felt something, like I was going to do something great in this world. But I didn't know what it was. But I was going to do it. And it seems that every work I got made my body stronger in a way. I just didn't know how. . . . But my body was built in a different way. . . . My muscles weren't built in a fitness room. My muscles were built with a lot of effort. . . . As a child, sometimes when I was working, my dad's bosses would tell him, "You can't make this boy work so hard." My dad would tell them, "No, he will make it. He is a man. If he wants to be a man in life, he will need to overcome anything, and he will make it, give him work and he will do it." . . . If you don't have to run after anything, or work for anything, how are you going to grow as a person and as a human being in life?[2]

To Get to the Promised Land, You May Have to Cross a Desert

The book of Exodus tells us that Moses lived for forty years in Egypt, alongside Pharaoh and his family. Moses had a deep understanding of the "wisdom of the Egyptians and was powerful in speech and action" (Acts 7:22). Later, he lived in the desert for forty years and overcame new challenges.

When Moses received God's command to lead the people of Israel out of slavery in Egypt, he tried to get out of it. But when he finally accepted his calling from God, Moses proved to be a great leader, one who is respected to this day by strategists and researchers. When the time came to free the

41

Hebrew people, Moses had already learned how the Egyptian government and institutions worked, and he knew how to live in the desert; these were precisely the two skills he would need.

Machiavelli said of Moses: "But to come to those who, by their own ability and not through fortune, have risen to be princes, I say that Moses, Cyrus, Romulus, Theseus, and such like are the most excellent examples. And although one may not discuss Moses, he having been a mere executor of the will of God, yet he ought to be admired, if only for that favour which made him worthy to speak with God."[3]

Moses's case is fascinating for three reasons.

First, Moses led a people who said they preferred to live in slavery rather than pay the price of freedom. It is not easy to wake up from a state of lethargy when life is neither totally good nor entirely bad. Many people resign themselves to an inferior personal, professional, emotional, or financial situation instead of doing something to change it. Unem- ←
ployment, underemployment, low wages, and debt are also forms of slavery, and breaking free requires planning, action, and patience in order to reap the results.

Second, when everything seemed lost, some of the people wanted to commit suicide, another group thought about returning to slavery, and a third group asked for Moses's head. At that point, Moses showed faith in God and began praying, as we saw in the Law of Faith. When he asked God for help, Moses received a harsh response from the Lord: "Why are you crying out to me? Tell the people to get moving!" (Exod. 14:15 NLT). The lesson here is that there is a time to retreat in prayer and a time to take action. The sea opens for those who march in its direction.

Third, refusing to settle and deciding to break free from slavery requires a willingness to face obstacles. Moses and the people of Israel confronted their own complacency; they also faced Pharaoh, his army, the sea, the desert, a long period of wandering, and finally even the inhabitants of the promised land. It was no small endeavor, but it was worth it. As we remind our students in our workshops about how to pass tests and public service exams: "To get to the promised land, you may have to cross a desert."

If you dream of a land "of milk and honey" (Exod. 33:3 NIrV), prepare yourself for a long journey. It is hard work and takes time, but it pays off.

The bitter past, more welcome is the sweet.

Shakespeare

FOUR

The Law of Well-Rewarded Affliction

Tribulation produces perseverance.

Romans 5:3 NKJV

There is nothing inviting about the word *affliction*. But without a good dose of it, rarely does anyone attain great victories. Athletes understand the expression "no pain, no gain." Affliction refers to the long period of difficulties, suffering, and frustration we must endure until the results of our efforts are recognized and rewarded.

Because the marketplace is tough and demanding, often we are required to endure unpleasant situations. But we need to believe that this effort will be recognized and rewarded. On the spiritual level, the development of our skills depends on overcoming challenges, and the affliction that we face often has strong educational content. In order to train us, our more experienced partner, God, places obstacles along the way for us to overcome.

The story of Jacob, told in Genesis 25–49, illustrates important lessons about the Law of Well-Rewarded Affliction. Jacob was a mistreated employee, exploited by his father-in-law, Laban. This young man tolerated all kinds of troubles because of his love for Rachel, Laban's youngest daughter. The poet Luís de Camões eternalized this love in his sonnet "Jacob": "For seven years, the shepherd Jacob slaved for the father of beautiful Rachel, working not for the man, but only for her, knowing ever since he began that she alone was the only reward he craved."[1]

Jacob was deceived by Rachel's father. Even though he had agreed to work for seven years for the dowry of his beloved Rachel, when the time was up, on his wedding day, Laban gave Jacob his older daughter, Leah, instead. Jacob's scheming father-in-law made him work another seven years for the right to marry his favorite. The shepherd accepted the sacrifice and, in the words of Camões, "If life wasn't so short, beginning right now, I'd serve even longer for Rachel, the love of my life."[2]

The conflict between Jacob and Laban serves as a warning about the importance of discussing and documenting all agreements you make. Don't be afraid or embarrassed to spell out the conditions of a contract, including clauses to protect yourself against potential future problems (including the famous *way out*, a clause about how to undo a business deal or partnership in the case of disagreements or litigation). If Jacob had been more careful when he had agreed on the dowry with Laban, he wouldn't have been deceived.

It is worth noting ~~that~~ Jacob himself had been devious earlier in life when he tricked his father and brother. This is worthy of attention: eventually all scoundrels are confronted with someone even more devious than themselves. Scoundrels often think ~~that~~ everyone is a fool—until someone cheats them. Or they are unmasked, and people quit doing business with them. Either way, it's not worth it.

After serving fourteen years for Laban's two daughters, Jacob continued working another six for his father-in-law in a rural partnership until he decided to leave. By that time, Jacob had become wealthier than Laban. How did this happen? His father-in-law had stopped working, allowing Jacob to take care of everything. Laban's case is one of someone who goes from success to failure, someone who gets lazy and pays a high price for his attitude.

It's worth remembering ~~that~~ success and failure apply to ✳ situations, not to people. Never say, "I am a failure"; instead, say, "This deal was a failure" or "I failed in this endeavor." Don't look at your failures as the end of the world; consider them as opportunities to learn something new. Nor should you go around saying, "I am a success." Even though you may have been successful here or there, don't become arro- ✳ gant, because your situation can change any minute. Both the good times and the bad times will pass. And never lose sight of the fact ~~that~~ it is God who gives us the strength to ✳ acquire wealth.

Laban's problem is common in the lives of many business owners we have met. As soon as the company starts making money, these owners leave everything in the hands of a manager and head to the beach. If the manager is dishonest, the company's downfall will be quick. But even if the person in charge has integrity, the owner must be involved in his business. After all, as a popular Brazilian saying goes, "The eye of the master fattens his cattle."

If all the know-how is concentrated in the hands of the manager, the company will find itself in a vulnerable position, for the manager could get an offer from a competitor, leave for personal reasons, or decide to open their own business. One way to deal with managers' natural desires for growth is to give them a share in the profits. However, no matter how well businesspeople take care of their employees, there is no way to avoid the risk of losing them. The following Biblical concepts should be applied here: "Know the state of your flocks, and put your heart into caring for your herds" (Prov. 27:23 NLT) and "Through laziness, the rafters sag; because of idle hands, the house leaks" (Eccles. 10:18).

How to Handle Situations of Exploitation

Important research shows that the longest-lasting companies are those that treat their employees and clients fairly. In their book *Built to Last*, Jim Collins and Jerry Porras, assisted by a team of twenty researchers from Stanford University, compared a group of enduring companies—which resisted the test of time and stayed on top—with other companies that didn't make it very long. The companies that last, those considered "visionaries," have strong cultures that guide their actions; at the same time they invest in progress, improvements, and innovation. "A visionary company creates a total environment that envelops employees, bombarding them with a set of signals so consistent and mutually reinforcing that it's virtually impossible to misunderstand the company's ideology and ambitions."[3]

We have also noticed that those who exploit others, such as Laban did, often end up badly. Exploiting others is not a long-lasting process. Are there people who exploit others and still do okay? Yes, but we believe that these are exceptions; the general rule is that such a system will not bear good fruit. Perhaps if Laban had built a healthy relationship with Jacob rather than exploiting him, Laban's story would have had a different ending.

During their partnership, however, Laban created an environment of dissatisfaction that led to the dissolution of the relationship. Here is what Jacob said to his wives, Laban's daughters: "You know that with all my might I have served your father. Yet your father has deceived me and changed my wages ten times, but God did not allow him to hurt me" (Gen. 31:6–7 NKJV).

Each time that Laban changed Jacob's salary, with the intent of being more successful and raising profits, he was undermining the trust between the two, the *affectio societatis*—in other words, the willingness to maintain the partnership. This legal term refers to partners, but we use it here in the relationship between boss and employee because it is a clear reflection of the ~~wish~~ ^{desire} to maintain a commercial and professional relationship—as a supplier, client, employee, or boss. Jacob was extremely tolerant until he decided ~~that~~ he had suffered enough exploitation. After <u>all</u>, he knew how to manage the business better than his father-in-law. The one who came out on the losing end was Laban, who lost a loyal and efficient worker.

Jacob attributed to God the fact ~~that~~ he wasn't completely ruined. We can attest ~~that~~ God does intervene in this way, ultimately rewarding those who are <u>faithful</u> to Him. But even if we set aside divine intervention, it is undeniable ~~that~~ work itself has a transformative power and ~~that~~ people will always profit from what they <u>learn</u> even when not being valued or not receiving what is fair.

We imagine ~~that~~ one of Laban's greatest frustrations was being far away from his daughters and grandchildren when Jacob left. But he was responsible for what happened. The following passage serves as a warning: "Whoever digs a pit will fall into it; and whoever breaks through a wall will be bitten by a snake" (Eccles. 10:8 NRSV). The Law of Sowing (described in *The 25 Biblical Laws of Success*) comes into play full force here. Laban reaped what he sowed, including his daughters' estrangement. If Laban hadn't deceived his son-in-law and imposed marriage with Leah, Jacob would not have left, or if he had, he would have taken only Rachel.

As this story exemplifies well, even competent professionals undergo trials in their careers. Due to great pressure over <u>time</u>, we have the potential to transform into diamonds. Being exploited or humiliated is a terrible experience, but it can help us build solid bases and pursue even more challenging goals. We need to be prepared for life's inevitable injustices because the winds will not always be in our favor. We should allow hardships to strengthen us.

In *The Art of Worldly Wisdom*, writer Baltasar Gracián, who influenced thinkers and philosophers, recommends knowing how to wait: "It's a sign of a noble heart dowered with patience, never to be in a hurry, never to be in a passion. You must pass through the circumference of time before arriving at the centre of opportunity."[4] Never sacrifice your values; be honest, virtuous, and friendly. Treat others as you would like to be treated, give more than you need to give, don't cheat anyone, and be tolerant, competent, and hardworking. Be ready to face injustices and affliction. This does not mean that you should submit to insults, exploitation, and psychological or sexual harassment. Take appropriate action to defend yourself from illegal behavior, and if necessary, quit your job and file a lawsuit. But be careful not to become too impatient to the point of being considered difficult or oversensitive.

The Scriptures challenge us to a life of resistance and courage: "If racing against mere men makes you tired, how will you race against horses? If you stumble and fall on open ground, what will you do in the thickets near the Jordan?" (Jer. 12:5 NLT).

The river reaches its goals because it has learned to get around obstacles.

LAO-TZU

FIVE

The Law of the Garden

In every place where I cause My name to be remembered, I will come to you and bless you.

Exodus 20:24 NASB

Thrive in the soil in which you were planted. As poet Mario Quintana wrote, "The secret is not to take care of the butterflies, but to take care of the garden so the butterflies come to you."[1] Make your garden more beautiful, whatever it may be. The butterflies will come—sometimes in order to improve your salary or position and other times to invite you to be a gardener in another place.

In every situation, your remarkable and one-of-a-kind partner—God—will accompany you. According to the Law of Training (see chapter 3), if God doesn't change the circumstances, He may want to either change you or give you the privilege of serving Him. In this case, you need to do a good

51

✳ job right where you are, trusting God; at the right moment He will provide the change. After all, God "changes the times and the seasons; He removes kings and raises up kings; He gives wisdom to the wise and knowledge to those who have understanding" (Dan. 2:21 NKJV).

Looking for better places to work or new opportunities for growth is not forbidden, of course. But those who change jobs frequently and jump from pasture to pasture, believing that the grass is always greener on the other side, will find that this attitude may get in the way of motivation, focus, and productivity. Instead, reflect on the possibility that God ✳ may have placed you where you are to accomplish some mission, to do your best for others, and to defend eternal principles and values.

The Law of the Garden should not be confused with complacency. It has a spiritual dimension that produces acceptance and service. When the people of Israel went into exile, the prophet Jeremiah told them to work for the good of the place to which they were going. Note that they were going as slaves! When we look at two different Bible translations of Jeremiah 29:7, the depth of the message is clear: "Work for the peace and prosperity of the city where I sent you into exile. Pray to the LORD for it, for its welfare ✳ will determine your welfare" (NLT). "Seek the peace of the city where I have caused you to be carried away captive, and pray to the LORD for it; for in its peace you will have peace" (NKJV).

Understanding that God is in control involves accepting that sometimes we face a hard situation in life, either as a result of what we have sown or due to a divine decision. ✓ Hence, even if only out of submission to God, we need to be fully there. If we want to change, the <u>first</u> step is to understand ~~that~~ in order to be transplanted, a plant must <u>first</u> be strong. The harder you work in the garden in which you have been placed, the easier it will be for you to grow and, in the future, the better <u>opportunity</u> you will have of being transferred to and thriving in a more fertile land.

It is common for some people to say ~~that~~ⁿ if they only had a good <u>opportunity</u>, they would dedicate themselves to their tasks and do an excellent job." But while they wait for some twist of fate, they don't put even a little effort into their daily tasks, and they waste a real <u>opportunity</u> to prove their talent. Meanwhile, people committed to working hard wherever they are will soon distinguish themselves. It is no coincidence ~~that~~ the best <u>opportunities</u> appear to this second group.

The Law of the Garden versus Marketing 3.0

The Law of the Garden can be summed up in the following way: while you are in one place, work to make it better. ✓ This idea is in accordance with the concepts put forward by marketing guru Philip Kotler.

Kotler shows the evolution that has occurred in the market. Marketing 1.0, from the era of the Industrial Revolution, had as its objective selling products. Then came the Information Technology era, Marketing 2.0, which was <u>focused</u> on satisfying and retaining consumers. Today, marketing is centered on values and human beings. According to Kotler,
service

we are in Marketing 3.0, where the focus is on making the world a better place.[2] *Serving*

In Marketing 1.0, the company focused on the product; in Marketing 2.0, the company focused on the consumer; and in Marketing 3.0, the company is focused on values. Companies saw the markets first as mass consumers, then as intelligent people endowed with hearts and minds, and lastly, as complete human beings, each with a heart, mind, and spirit.

Along this line, the concept of marketing has evolved from mere product development to differentiation to human values. The value proposition evolved from merely functional in 1.0, to functional in 2.0, and to emotional and spiritual in 3.0. Currently the interaction with consumers is considered an action of "one for many."

If you apply these concepts to your professional life, then you will stand out—not only because you're in touch with the most modern marketing ideas today, but also because you're in tune with the Bible's ancient wisdom, which invests above all in people and values.

Life isn't about waiting for the storm to pass.
It's about learning to dance in the rain.

VIVIAN GREENE

PART 2

Laws
concerning
Effort

SIX

The Law
of Maximum Quality

Bondservants, be obedient to those who are your
masters according to the flesh, with fear and trem-
bling, in sincerity of heart, as to Christ; not with
eyeservice, as men-pleasers, but as bondservants
of Christ, doing the will of God from the heart,
with goodwill doing service, as to the Lord, and
not to men, knowing ~~that~~ whatever good anyone does, he will receive the same from the Lord,
whether he is a slave or free.

And you, masters, do the same things to them,
giving up threatening, knowing ~~that~~ your own
Master also is in heaven, and there is no partiality with Him.

Ephesians 6:5–9 NKJV

The Bible proposes a commitment of maximum quality: work as though the receiver of your service were God Him-self. Whether you are creating a product, assisting a client, studying, or working, your focus should be this special part-ner. God does not demand that you be a financial genius or a superhero, but He expects that you work toward the highest standard when it comes to your attitudes and behavior. You should willingly fulfill your responsibilities with goodwill, care, and dedication, regardless of whether you are being observed by your boss.

The Bible text that opens this chapter uses the term *ser-vants*, but in today's terms, *employees* would be more ap-propriate. Yet we cannot lose sight of the original meaning: even in the context of slavery, the command is to work with dedication and care. Even when the employer was not a good person, the servant or slave must endeavor to work as if they were serving Jesus.

Today this seems outrageous. On the one hand, young people who are entering the job market are much more aware of their rights and are not willing to work for bosses who do not know how to recognize their efforts and talent or who exploit or humiliate them. On the other hand, there is a rule of conduct, of common sense, of cordiality and fulfilling your duty that is still relevant: no matter what po-sition you are in, obey your superior. Be faithful to whom you serve, whether it's the government, the owner of the company where you work, or your majority partner in a busi-ness. Sometimes the "boss" will be the contract you signed; respect what was agreed on. This principle only ceases to be valid if your boss demands ~~that~~ you do something wrong, unethical, or dishonest.

If you are a public servant, do your job with dignity. Remember ~~that~~, ultimately, you are not working for the government. The real recipient of your service is other people, the population as a whole. Strive for a genuine desire to do the best for those whom you have an obligation to serve. It may seem like a paradigm shift, but imagine what would happen if this became the norm.

Don't use your boss as an excuse not to work productively and efficiently. Bad employers and governments are not justifications for you not to do your part. Keep in mind ~~that~~ your most important contract is with God. The best results of everything you do in your life will not come from your superiors; they will be the fruit of what you plant as an ethical person.

Good professionals, especially leaders, always work for something bigger than themselves. Whether it is to change the world, to create something new, or to honor God, there must be some greater motive for great things to happen. This type of mission will allow people to grow. Nothing will be done with maximum quality if it is motivated by small thinking.

The book *Dream Big*, written by journalist Cristiane Correa, shows how the search for excellence and a culture of meritocracy guided the successful careers of the Brazilian businessmen Jorge Paulo Lemann, Marcel Telles, and Beto Sicupira. The trio built the biggest empire in the history of Brazilian capitalism and gained world recognition by buying three icons of American culture: Budweiser, Burger King, and Heinz. The expression that became the title of the book was used by Lemann when he talked about how Harvard changed his vision of the world, making him more ambitious in life: "Most people who know me and are aware of my businesses, know that I always say that having a big dream generates the same amount of work as having a little dream."[1]

Dream big. It doesn't matter whether you are sweeping the floor, reconstructing a tooth, teaching a class, or leading a major corporation: seek excellence. Better yet, work as if you were doing it for God. The result will be that you will do an even better job. To God, all work is worthy, sacred, and useful; even the humblest activity should be valued and well-executed. Teachers, consultants, and specialists in the most diverse areas affirm the extraordinary effort to work for something bigger than yourself. And there is nothing bigger than God or more important than serving Him. Hence, practicing the Law of Maximum Quality will reveal a high degree not only of spiritual elevation but also of sophistication from the secular point of view.

People who perform their best work willingly, rather than forcibly or reluctantly, tend to be admired and well liked. Even though you shouldn't work merely to seek recognition, the truth is that sooner or later recognition will come to those who dedicate themselves, body and soul, to the job. The Law of Maximum Quality has two immediate effects:

1. A secular reward, since by implementing it you will reach a higher level of excellence at work.

2. A divine promise, since you will be <u>faithful</u> and obe- ✓
   dient to God, and this never goes unnoticed in the
   eyes of the Father.

Furthermore, you will receive a priceless reward: a clear
conscience and the sense of a job well done.

Maximum Quality in Charge

Those who are at the top of the hierarchy should also, in
relation to their subordinates, act as if they are dealing with
God. Would the owner or manager of a company that had
Jesus as an employee treat Him with rudeness or disrespect
or fail to give Him His worker's rights? We don't think so.
And according to Biblical recommendation, no one deserves
to be treated like that. In the Bible passage quoted at the beginning of this chapter, the "masters"—employers—should
also act this way with their employees. The Biblical text
warns bosses not to make threats or show partiality—in
other words, not to benefit some employees to the detriment
of others, based on social class, titles, and the like.

If you are a manager, director, or owner of a company and
think that you can do whatever you want with your employees, remember that up above there is a Boss who is superior
to you. Even if you don't <u>believe</u> in God, you are certainly
capable of understanding that treating your employees well
will make them more motivated and committed.

Some people think you have to treat relatives, children, students, or employees with an excess of discipline and authority;

otherwise, they will take advantage of you or the situation. This is an often-heard theory, and you have the right to be-lieve it because everyone has the right to err. The problem is that you will suffer the consequences of this type of mistaken behavior.

Do superiors have complete freedom to act however they want with their inferiors? Of course not. They are limited by legal obligations that require proper and fair treatment of employees. The Law of Maximum Quality goes beyond ✓ the human view of justice and recommends that bosses treat ∕ their employees as they would treat Jesus. But even if company owners, executives, or managers apply only the Golden Rule and treat others as they would like to be treated (Matt. 7:12), this would remedy the problem.

Whether you are at the top, in the middle, or at the bottom of the pyramid, you should act respectfully in all your ⅄ commercial and professional relations. Treat your boss well, treat your employees well, and treat your partners, clients, and suppliers well. But don't do that to please others or ✓ ingratiate yourself to them. Always remember that you are actually your own boss. It's as if you are a company, and you're working to make it grow.

Maximum Quality versus Minimum Quality

What if you disrespect others? What if you ignore the Law of Maximum Quality? You will certainly suffer the consequences of the Law of Sowing (described in *The 25 Biblical Laws of Success*). "Anyone who does wrong will be repaid for their wrongs, and there is no favoritism" (Col. 3:25). Our world keeps on turning, so what goes around comes around. Don't forget this when you consider treating someone badly.

It would be ideal if you could say, like Paul, "We have wronged no one, we have corrupted no one, we have exploited no one" (2 Cor. 7:2). It is impossible to grow within a Biblical framework if you are exploiting others. It is not worth walking the paths of injustice—such attitudes produce resentment and the desire for revenge, and they will destroy any company or team.

This issue isn't only about how we treat others. The way we speak to colleagues and subordinates counts as well. Solomon says, "A gentle answer turns away wrath, but a harsh word stirs up anger" (Prov. 15:1); "Anxiety in a man's heart weighs it down, but a good word makes it glad" (Prov. 12:25 NASB); "A person finds joy in giving an apt reply— and how good is a timely word!" (Prov. 15:23); and "Sweetness of the lips increases learning" (Prov. 16:21 NKJV). If you want a more productive team, learn to communicate effectively.

Even those who don't believe in the existence of a just God should be careful of their actions. Aside from the spiritual consequences of treating employees disrespectfully, there are labor lawsuits, losses associated with excessive turnover of employees, and even sabotage committed by disgruntled, unmotivated employees. Not to mention the negative image that unfair, rude, and unethical behavior can bring to you and your company. Nobody can hide who they really are from everyone all the time.

Businesspeople, executives, and managers should not forget the important marketing principle that customer satisfaction is directly proportional to the satisfaction of company employees. If you wish to discover how much your customers are satisfied with your company, simply measure how much your employees are satisfied with your company. We suggest that you evaluate, maybe even by using a third party and/or questionnaires, what the members of your team actually think about you and your company.

If you want to take the Law of Maximum Quality beyond your professional life, ask your spouse, children, and friends to tell you with absolute sincerity what they think of you. Prepare to deal with their responses and to make the adjustments that will help you grow as a person.

Life is a grindstone. But whether it grinds us down or polishes us up depends on us.
L. Thomas Holdcroft

SEVEN

The Law of the Extra Mile

> If someone slaps you on the right cheek, offer the
> other cheek also. If you are sued in court and your
> shirt is taken from you, give your coat, too. If a
> soldier demands ~~that~~ you carry his gear for a mile,
> carry it two miles. Give to those who ask, and
> don't turn away from those who want to borrow.
>
> Matthew 5:39–42 NLT

A successful business is not built by people who limit themselves to the bare minimum. The basics—the required tasks ~~that~~ everyone does (or should do)—are just the starting point. Extraordinary companies and professionals are those who go above and beyond the rest, exceeding expectations.

This is precisely the focus of the Law of the Extra Mile. Those who are idle and careless are a mile behind, and the average person is exactly at the mile marker—in other words, they only do what is expected of them. But the above-average professional is a mile ahead.

In Matthew 5:39–42, Jesus talked about how to deal with people who require others to do what they themselves don't want to do. Even in these cases, Christ proposed that we go beyond what is expected. Accountability or obligation notwithstanding, the willingness to deliver more than is requested or officially demanded can be advantageous in the business world.

In his book *Please Don't Just Do What I Tell You! Do What Needs to Be Done*, business consultant Bob Nelson explained that this proactive attitude is a mark of professional excellence and the edge that every boss looks for in a team. Since not all companies clearly define their expectations for employees, Nelson summarized employers' key expectations: "We hired you to do the job; however, more importantly, we hired you to think, to use your discernment and act according to the company's interests at all times. Always do what most needs to be done without waiting to be asked."[1]

Napoleon Hill made the same point in his classic book, *The Law of Success in Sixteen Lessons*: "If you want to stand out in your field of work, you need to create the healthy habit of walking the extra mile: always do more than they ask, always do more than is required of you. Otherwise, you will only be a mediocre person, like so many others."[2] According to Hill, there are two types of people who don't get ahead:

1. Those who don't do what is asked of them.
2. Those who do only what is asked of them.

The professional who stays and looks over a finished project one more _time_ instead of handing it in and leaving work on _time_ is sure to impress. And the same goes for those who add a special extra touch to their work, going beyond the call of duty.

Promise less, and deliver more. This is the higher grade of excellence that everyone can _practice_, but few do. We _hope_ you are one of the few.

"It's Not My Responsibility"

Nobody can tolerate employees or companies ~~that~~ who avoid doing what they could by claiming, "It's not my responsibility." Organizations that provide good service stand out because of employees who make an effort to resolve clients' problems, going beyond what is required of them. Consumers perceive this as an invaluable asset.

In the parable of the good Samaritan as recorded in Luke 10 (NRSV), Jesus told the story of a Samaritan—a member of a group discriminated against by the Jews for not having pure Hebrew blood—who helped a wounded man on the road. Shortly beforehand, a priest and a Levite—two religious men—passed by the injured man and didn't do anything to help him.

Was it their responsibility to help a stranger? The parable was Jesus's answer to an expert in religious law who put him to the test by asking, "Teacher, what must I do to inherit eternal life?" (v. 25). Jesus asked the lawyer what was written in the law, and the lawyer responded, "Love the Lord your God with all your heart and with all your soul and with all your strength and with all your mind'; and, 'Love your neighbor as yourself'" (v. 27). Then to justify himself, the man asked, "And who is my neighbor?" (v. 29).

Here is Jesus's reply:

> A man was going down from Jerusalem to Jericho, and fell into the hands of robbers, who stripped him, beat him, and went away, leaving him half dead. Now by chance a priest was going down that road; and when he saw him, he passed by on the other side. So likewise, a Levite, when he came to the place and saw him, passed by on the other side. But a Samaritan while traveling came near him; and when he saw him, he was moved with pity. He went to him and bandaged his wounds, having poured oil and wine on them. Then he put him on his own animal, brought him to an inn, and took care of him. The next day he took out two denarii, gave them to the innkeeper, and said, "Take care of him; and when I come back, I will repay you whatever more you spend." Which of these three, do you think, was a neighbor to the man who fell into the hands of the robbers? (vv. 30–36)

Jesus's parable ended with the law expert admitting, "The one who had mercy on him" (v. 37). And Jesus made a simple recommendation: "Go and do likewise" (v. 37).

This parable illustrates important lessons that not only apply to our careers but also teach us to be better people. The irony of the story is that it was the Samaritan, a person who was looked down on by society, who demonstrated mercy, solidarity, and generosity toward the injured man. And even more curious is the fact that the Samaritan appeared to be a man of means, maybe even a businessman, but he applied the Biblical laws of partnership with God better than the two men who viewed themselves as religious individuals.

The good Samaritan followed several of the Biblical laws of success as well. He was concerned about others. He was well prepared, having brought wine and oil. He was also organized and appeared to have a good life plan. He had probably allowed plenty of time to travel, and that is why he could go to the inn and stay for a day. He paid in advance the equivalent of two nights' stay, and, since he was a trustworthy man, the owner of the inn let him put future expenses on his bill to be paid later.

This incredible story about mercy and loving your neighbor has as its backdrop a man of means who was organized and trustworthy. Despite his wealth, he showed concern for an injured stranger and took care of him. Jesus used the Samaritan as a paradigm for the qualities that we suggest in *The 25 Biblical Laws of Success* and in this book.

We ain't what we want to be; we ain't what
we ought to be; we ain't what we gonna be,
but thank God, we ain't what we was.

MARTIN LUTHER KING JR., QUOTING
AN OLD AFRICAN AMERICAN SLAVE PREACHER

EIGHT

The Law of Entrepreneurship

When he had spent everything, a severe famine
occurred in that country, and he began to be impoverished. So he went and hired himself out to
one of the citizens of that country.

Luke 15:14–15 NASB

Many young people dream of winning the lottery, inheriting
a fortune from a distant relative, or getting an invitation to
be a partner or manager in the coolest company they can
think of. Newspapers report cases of the meteoric success
of people who were in the right place at the right time, and
films show fairy-tale marriages that change people's lives
from one day to the next, bringing them not only love but
also wealth.

Many people believe they would do well if only luck would smile on them or if God would perform some kind of miracle in their lives. Unfortunately, this type of behavior causes a kind of paralysis and, instead of sowing opportunities and getting ready to reap future results, they sit and wait for something to fall from the sky.

How many people would be successful if they had the courage to act, experiment, and take risks? And even if they didn't have immediate success, wouldn't it be better to try and to fail than to be stuck in the same spot? The answer, once again, is in the Bible. One of the most well-known and studied of Jesus's stories is the parable of the prodigal son about an unsatisfied young man who lived on his father's farm and took his part of the inheritance and went in search of new personal and professional challenges.

Here is the story Jesus told:

A man had two sons. The younger of them said to his father, "Father, give me the share of the estate that falls to me." So he divided his wealth between them. And not many days later, the younger son gathered everything together and went on a journey into a distant country, and there he squandered his estate with loose living. Now when he had spent everything, a severe famine occurred in that country, and he began to be impoverished. So he went and hired himself out to one of the citizens of that country, and he sent him into his fields to feed swine. And he would have gladly filled his stomach with the pods that the swine were eating, and no one was giving anything to him. But when he came to his senses, he said, "How many of my father's hired men have more than enough bread, but I am dying here with hunger! I will get up and go to my father, and will say to him, 'Father, I have sinned against heaven, and in your sight; I am no longer worthy to be called your son; make me as one of your hired men.'" So he got up and came to his father. But while he was still a long way off, his father saw him and felt compassion for him, and ran and embraced him and kissed him. And the son said to him, "Father, I have sinned against heaven and in your sight; I am no longer worthy to be called your son." But the father said to his slaves, "Quickly bring out the best robe and put it on him, and put a ring on his hand and sandals on his feet; and bring the fattened calf, kill it, and let us eat and celebrate; for this son of mine was dead and has come to life again; he was lost and has been found." And they began to celebrate.

Now his older son was in the field, and when he came and approached the house, he heard music and dancing. And he summoned one of the servants and began inquiring what these things could be. And he said to him, "Your brother has come, and your father has killed the fattened calf because he has received him back safe and sound." But he became angry and was not willing to go in; and his father came out and began pleading with him. But he answered and said to his father, "Look! For so many years I have been serving you and I have never neglected a command of yours; and yet you have never given me a young goat, so that I might celebrate with my friends; but when this son of yours came, who has devoured your wealth with prostitutes, you killed the fattened calf for him." And he said to him, "Son, you have always been with me, and all that is mine is yours. But we had to celebrate and rejoice, for this brother of yours was dead and has begun to live, and was lost and has been found." (Luke 15:11–32 NASB)

This parable, which perhaps should be named "Two Lost Sons," offers the most diverse teachings, showing the mistakes and successes of the two boys. In general, people think ~~that~~ the son who went away was the bad one and the son who stayed was the good one, but that's not exactly how it was.

The Younger Son versus the Older Son

The younger son in Jesus's parable had many of the features common to humanity. He was dissatisfied and wanted more out of life. Many people feel that way, with some resigning themselves to their circumstances and others taking action. The prodigal son was part of the group that didn't just resign themselves. Score one for him.

The problem was ~~that~~ this young man, even though he was the son of a successful and experienced businessman, did ✓ not prepare himself for the challenges ahead. He didn't get advice from his dad or try to learn from him how to manage his wealth, how to choose good business partners, and how to distinguish friends from enemies. From the height of his arrogance, he simply asked for his part of the inheritance and left.

The younger son's lack of financial discipline and inability to negotiate caused him to lose everything. When there is plenty of money and a favorable market, we often can't see our own vulnerability. S̲uccess masks o̲ur w̲eaknesses. Those who are on top run the risk of being overly confident and neglecting the basics that helped them get there. Warren Buffett, one of the richest men in the world, said, "It's only when the tide goes out that you discover who's been swimming naked."[1]

The young heir in Jesus's story was certainly "swimming naked." He didn't have the w̲isdom to seek knowledge from his father before going off in search of his dreams. Worse yet, he offended his dad, wasted his fortune, and got involved with people who were interested only in his money. However, despite his mistakes, the prodigal son had some useful characteristics to succeed in life. He was an entrepreneur—and it is entrepreneurs who change the world. The prodigal son devised a plan and rolled up his sleeves, ready to begin: he asked for his inheritance and left home to try his luck. He didn't do it in the best way because he disrespected his dad and was arrogant, but at least he wasn't just dead weight, doing nothing while complaining about his life.

When everything went wrong, the prodigal son didn't sink into depression or sit around whining. Instead, he found work in order to survive. His actions are worthy of merit. Furthermore, when he found himself among the pigs—hungry, unhappy, defeated, and certainly mulling over his mistakes—he didn't give up. He devised a new plan and executed it.

The prodigal son's willingness to face difficulties in his pursuit of fulfillment helped him to l̲earn and grow. Despite ending up in a pigsty, he discovered ~~that~~ he had been happy but didn't know it. So with newfound maturity, he was willing to admit his failure to his father and humbly accept a subordinate position, which would still be better than the pigsty from which he had come.

If given the same circumstances as the prodigal son, many people would spend their entire lives complaining, others would give up, and still others would allow their pride to keep them from asking for a position on their father's farm—but not that young man. He moved into action. Those who take up the fight will face both good and bad situations and will have either good or bad luck. The prodigal son was ~~lucky~~ blessed to be received by his father in a way he could never have imagined. He didn't even have to listen to a lecture! What kind of father is that? The father in Jesus's parable was a wonderful father, modeled on the heavenly Father.

We should <u>learn</u> not only from the prodigal son's mistakes but also from his successes. His entrepreneurship and <u>courage</u> to take risks and make plans to try to achieve his goals made him grow as a person. At the end of his long journey in search of happiness, he returned to the same place he had left, but he had <u>learned</u> the value of what he had.

The older brother in Jesus's story, considered by many to be the victim of the situation, was bitter and spiteful. In fact, Jesus told this parable to comment on the older brother's attitude—namely, his lack of forgiveness regarding his younger brother's mistakes. The older brother also offended his father, since he didn't respect his father's decisions, refusing even to participate in the party celebrating his brother's return.

The firstborn apparently felt like a slave in his house and didn't take advantage of what his father had to offer. He complained that he had never partied with his friends, and his father was surprised, saying, that everything he had also belonged to his son. The young man could have organized a party if he had desired, but he never did.

In the same way, many people feel like slaves rather than owners of their work, their studies, or their marriage, which compromises not only their joy of living but also their productivity. The worst part is that those who act like this waste the opportunities they have been given.

Comparing the two sons, we see that the younger son, who acted like an entrepreneur by making plans and going after his dreams, was the one who truly progressed, even though he made mistakes and suffered for them. The older son did not follow the Law of Entrepreneurship. Stop and consider this: Have you behaved like one of the sons in the parable? Try not to make the same mistakes they did.

Employability versus Entrepreneurship

There is a difference between employability and entrepreneurship. It is one thing to be employable—in other words, to be someone with the right qualifications and desirable market skills. It is another thing to be an entrepreneur who is willing to start new businesses or projects. All employees, especially leaders, should show initiative and be innovative.

But not everyone will be entrepreneurs in the strict sense of the term.

The market has room for both good entrepreneurs and good employees. There are many different models of professional success, and not everyone wants to start a multinational company in their garage.

Even if you are not an entrepreneur, you need to realize ~~that~~ those who start a business need a team to help them. One of the ways to accumulate wealth is by assisting the entrepreneur. If you are not the owner but have qualifications ~~that are~~ useful for the business, you could have good opportunities for growth. If you are an entrepreneur but don't have the necessary skills, you will need to find a partner with those skills or hire someone who has them. In general, entrepreneurs do not possess all the abilities needed to make their businesses take off. That is why they need to evaluate people, hire them, and lead them in day-to-day tasks.

Or you may dream of passing an examination for a job in public service or of getting an MBA or another graduate degree. In each of these cases, you will need to associate with those who can help you and to make practical adjustments to face the new challenge.

Whether it is to build something new or to help those who do, you need to have positive attributes. What are yours? According to the Law of Employability (described in *The 25 Biblical Laws of Success*), the job market seeks people who are:

- Hard workers
- Competent
- Honest
- Pleasant

- ☑ Loyal and reliable
- ☑ Determined and persistent
- ☑ Patient
- ☑ Humble
- ☑ Team players
- ☑ Resilient

The prodigal son followed the Law of Entrepreneurship but not the Law of Employability. Do you think he was hardworking, competent, humble, and instilled with team spirit? So after losing his fortune—whether due to incompetence or to the drought that afflicted the region—this son had difficulty getting a good job in the marketplace. In the end, he was hired to take care of pigs, a job with no qualifications.

Not all companies go bankrupt due to the incompetence of an owner or manager. Sometimes businesses fail for other reasons, such as financial crises, changing times and technology, or just plain bad luck. The best manufacturer of horse whips ceased to be profitable after the invention of the automobile, just as the producers of typewriters went bankrupt after the advent of computers.

But the fact is that even in the biggest crises, and maybe even more so then, companies need talented and dedicated people who know how to motivate, produce, and create—in short, people capable of reversing negative situations. What skills do you have? Are you someone whom others seek out when they need to ask questions or get advice? In general, these people are the first to be promoted and, in a crisis, the last to be fired.

In conclusion, there is no use giving wealth or a job to someone who has not acquired the necessary skills or employable personal attributes. The Bible says, "It is senseless to pay to educate a fool, since he has no heart for learning" (Prov. 17:16 NLT).

Discontent is the first step in the
progress of a man or nation.

OSCAR WILDE

NINE

The Law of
the Favorable Impression

The good man brings out of his good treasure
what is good; and the evil man brings out of his
evil treasure what is evil.

Matthew 12:35 NASB

The impression you leave on people throughout life becomes either your greatest asset or your greatest liability. If you leave positive impressions in the minds of people, they will remember you fondly, and this will bring unexpected benefits.

In Jesus's parable of the prodigal son, which we analyzed in the Law of Entrepreneurship, the father waited anxiously for his youngest son's return, so much so that he waited on the porch, watching the road from which his son had left in hopes of seeing him again.

And why did the young man decide to return? Because his memory of his father was positive. He remembered his father as a good man who treated everyone well, including his employees. After reflecting on his father's generosity, in contrast to the pig farmer's greed, the prodigal son realized the mistake he had made: "How many of my father's hired servants have food to spare, and here I am starving to death!" (Luke 15:17). The father could not have imagined that by being good and <u>faithful</u> with his employees, he would be sowing the return of his son.

Joseph in Egypt, as we saw in the Law of Training, also faced <u>all</u> kinds of hardships on his journey, but he didn't abandon the path of integrity. He was sold into slavery by his own brothers and unjustly imprisoned, yet while in jail he helped many people without getting any recognition except from the jailer.

On one occasion, Pharaoh sent the palace chief cupbearer and chief baker to prison. While there, both men had upsetting dreams. Due to their anxiety, Joseph offered to interpret their dreams.

> The chief cupbearer told Joseph his dream. He said to him, "In my dream I saw a vine in front of me, and on the vine were three branches. As soon as it budded, it blossomed, and its clusters ripened into grapes. Pharaoh's cup was in my hand, and I took the grapes, squeezed them into Pharaoh's cup and put the cup in his hand."

"This is what it means," Joseph said to him. "The three branches are three days. Within three days Pharaoh will lift up your head and restore you to your position, and you will put Pharaoh's cup in his hand, just as you used to do when you were his cupbearer. But when all goes well with you, remember me and show me kindness; mention me to Pharaoh and get me out of this prison. I was forcibly carried off from the land of the Hebrews, and even here I have done nothing to deserve being put in a dungeon."

When the chief baker saw that Joseph had given a favorable interpretation, he said to Joseph, "I too had a dream: On my head were three baskets of bread. In the top basket were all kinds of baked goods for Pharaoh, but the birds were eating them out of the basket on my head."

"This is what it means," Joseph said. "The three baskets are three days. Within three days Pharaoh will lift off your head and impale your body on a pole. And the birds will eat away your flesh." (Gen. 40:9–19)

Joseph, using his gift of dream interpretation, accurately predicted both of their fates. The chief baker was hanged, and the cupbearer was restored to his office with Pharaoh. However, the cupbearer didn't remember Joseph's help and did not show gratitude to his prison mate. Two years later, when Pharaoh dreamed that seven fat cows went up to the river and were eaten by seven lean cows which had come after them, the cupbearer remembered Joseph's skills. Pharaoh sent for the prisoner, and Joseph correctly interpreted his dream. As a result, Joseph was put in charge of the whole land of Egypt.

In the end, people can fight against you, betray you, or abandon you, but they will never forget what you have left engraved in their minds. What records have you left in the minds of others?

You exist only in what you do.

Federico Fellini

TEN

The Law of Loving Leadership

There was also a dispute among them, as to which of them should be considered the greatest. And He said to them, "The kings of the Gentiles exercise lordship over them, and those who exercise authority over them are called 'benefactors.' But not so among you; on the contrary, he who is greatest among you, let him be as the younger, and he who governs as he who serves. For who is greater, he who sits at the table, or he who serves? Is it not he who sits at the table? Yet I am among you as the One who serves."

Luke 22:24–27 NKJV

The ability to lead is one of the attributes that will make the greatest impact on a professional's journey. All companies and organizations need leaders, but they especially need leaders who know how to use their charisma and their power for good—to make the world better—and not just for their own benefit. The Law of Loving Leadership goes one step further than the Law of Leadership, which we presented in *The 25 Biblical Laws of Success.*

We need to understand how to distinguish between different kinds of leaders. Adolph Hitler was a convincing and popular leader, capable of rounding up millions of people in support of Nazi ideology and his expansionist plans. His slogan was "One People, One Empire, One Leader." His leadership, however, was motivated by hate. Another example of a leader who caused death and destruction was the Reverend Jim Jones, founder of the cult the People's Temple. In the late 1970s, Jones ordered the mass suicide of the cult's Jonestown, Guyana, community. More than nine hundred people died, including children, most by poisoning.

Leadership doesn't only mean being followed but also taking people to a better place. Loving leadership is, above all, the ability to serve, not just to inspire or give orders. Gandhi was a great leader. Martin Luther King Jr. was a great leader. Nelson Mandela was a great leader. Jesus was the greatest leader who ever lived, and He left us a legacy of stories and teachings about loving and servant leadership.

The father described in Jesus's parable of the prodigal son (Luke 15:11–32), for example, can serve as a model of a loving leader. Check out some of his characteristics:

- He showed genuine interest in people.
- He was not easily offended by either of his sons.

85

- He didn't hold his sons back; instead, he gave them the freedom to follow their dreams.
- He wasn't attached to money (he gave the younger son's inheritance to him even though it wasn't legally required; he had the best calf served for the party; he made it clear that everything he owned also belonged to his sons).
- He was patient.
- He knew how to forgive.
- He didn't lecture or humiliate those who made mistakes.
- He knew how to celebrate good news.
- He adjusted his leadership style according to the behavior and personality of each person (he waited on the front porch for the younger son; he went outside to find his older son). He understood that there isn't a one-size-fits-all formula for getting along with others.
- He wasn't selfish.
- He was more concerned about people than things.
- He wanted his team (family and company) as a whole to be well; he had team spirit and motivated others to have this spirit as well.

To God, leadership is an important mission, for the leader's role is to serve and train people, especially new leaders.

We had the privilege of discussing leadership with Jorge Gerdau Johannpeter, chairman of the board of directors of the Gerdau Group. He shared several life lessons with us and said that if he could go back in time, he would give himself the same advice: be a servant leader. This answer shows the importance of loving leadership. He also stressed that a great leader should be concerned with all people, not just those who are considered more important. In addition, Gerdau addressed the importance of sustainability and family values. He said that he still follows his parents' advice: "Pay your bills on time, preferably a day before the deadline, to avoid any unforeseen glitches getting in the way of meeting the deadline."[1]

Nehemiah's Mission

Nehemiah is considered to be a successful person in the Bible, but what stands out the most to us in his story is his leadership ability alongside his sincere willingness to take risks for others.

In order to better understand the Old Testament character of Nehemiah, we need to know the setting in which he lived. The people of Judah had been taken into slavery by the king of Babylon. After seventy years in captivity, many returned to Jerusalem but were experiencing great difficulties because the city had been destroyed. The situation was discouraging.

Nehemiah, however, was privileged; even though he was a foreigner in Babylon, an exile, he was in a high social position because he was the cupbearer to King Artaxerxes. Although Nehemiah enjoyed a good position in Babylon, he was concerned about the situation of his home country and his people.

So Nehemiah decided to do the unimaginable: give up his position and his comfort in order to fulfill his dream of returning to Jerusalem.

It is said that luck is what happens when preparation meets opportunity. Some people are never prepared, which is the reason they rarely benefit from a chance occurrence. In Nehemiah's case, what came into play was not luck; it was divine providence. It was the combination of opportunity (given by God) and preparation. Nehemiah didn't simply go up to the king and ask to leave. He carefully prepared while he waited for an opportunity, and that is why he was successful in exposing Jerusalem's situation and his desire to do something for his people.

The king gave Nehemiah everything he needed to begin his new enterprise. He gave letters so Nehemiah could travel freely through the provinces until he arrived at Judah, and he also granted him authorization to obtain wood to rebuild Jerusalem. Undoubtedly, the fact that Nehemiah had exercised excellence in his job gave him the credibility to get what he wanted.

Nehemiah demonstrated humility by giving up a comfortable position to go to a place where there was confusion, pain, oppression, discouragement, corruption, mismanagement, and a lack of prospects. Only true leaders risk so much in the name of a cause or a new challenge.

To fulfill the mission he set for himself, Nehemiah had to deal with the envy of people living in the surrounding area who tried everything in their power to discourage him. But he refused to give up and became stronger as a leader, motivating his people and, in the end, successfully rebuilding the walls and gates of Jerusalem.

What can we learn from Nehemiah's example of loving leadership?

- Wherever you are, do your job with excellence.
- Don't become complacent when in a high position.
- When you are in situations of power, don't forget the poor and the needy.
- Don't be afraid to have bold dreams; think big.
- Prepare to transform your dream into reality.
- Never go to a meeting unprepared.
- Be humble, regardless of your position.
- Have the courage to fight for your goals.
- Find people who will help you to change reality.
- Know how to handle envy; the bigger your dream, the more envy it will generate.
- Create strategies to deal with obstacles.
- Develop your credibility.
- Be a self-motivator and a team motivator.

Lord, deliver me from everything that is devoid of love.
CAIO FERNANDO ABREU

PART 3

Laws
concerning
Righteousness

ELEVEN

The Law of Integrity

Blessed are the pure in heart, for they will see God.
Matthew 5:8 NRSV

Integrity has been defined as "the state of being whole and undivided."[1] It is also synonymous with character, honesty, and righteousness. Although integrity and honesty go together, we consider integrity a step beyond honesty. An honest person is wonderful, but some people go even further: they act with nobility, friendship, and loyalty toward all.

In the corporate world, having integrity is essential. Even the business magnate Warren Buffett, one of the richest and most successful people in the world, values this quality above all others when looking for potential business partners ("You can't make a good deal with a bad person"[2]) and when choosing the members of his team ("Somebody once said that in looking for people to hire, you look for three qualities:

integrity, intelligence, and energy. And if you don't have the first, the other two will kill you"[3]).

Similarly, in a partnership with God, integrity is an indispensable prerequisite. As British preacher Charles H. Spurgeon said, "Look you well to your integrity, and the Lord will look to your prosperity."[4] When we review the stories of success in the Bible, we see there is truth in this statement.

Be Loyal to Your Enemies

Consider the prophet Daniel, who was a model diplomat, cabinet minister, and public servant, as well as a paragon of faith. As we saw in the Law of Prayer, Daniel showed integrity not only in his relationship with God but also as a politician, public servant, and friend.

Daniel's story, as recorded in the Bible, began when Nebuchadnezzar, king of Babylon, conquered Jerusalem and took many Jews to serve in his palace. Daniel and his friends Hananiah, Mishael, and Azariah were chosen for the king's service because they were "showing intelligence in every branch of wisdom, endowed with understanding and discerning knowledge" (Dan. 1:4 NASB). In other words, the conquerors didn't choose just anyone to serve them. They chose the most prepared, proving that knowledge makes a difference even when we are at an absolute disadvantage.

At the palace, Daniel and his friends decided not to let themselves be contaminated by the environment or to compromise their values. This ethical stance could have put them at risk, for they refused the king's delicacies and wine. But the situation turned out well because Daniel and his friends were found to be healthier than everyone else and were called to serve King Nebuchadnezzar.

For those with principles, whether things go right or wrong is secondary. People of integrity act on the premise that principles cannot be negotiated. Such a viewpoint brings both advantages and disadvantages, admiration and hatred, opportunities and limitations. It is up to you to decide if you want to be like the majority and go with the flow or if you prefer to have nonnegotiable principles. The second option will make you stand out in the job market.

Daniel continued working as a wise man in the court. Some time later, Nebuchadnezzar had a dream that troubled him. He wanted the wise men of his kingdom to tell him what he had dreamed and to offer an interpretation. If they refused, he would kill them all. Daniel convinced the king to give him more time and asked him to spare the other wise men, showing his kind spirit. Daniel would not do evil just to become the king's only wise man. Unlike many people, Daniel knew that you don't build a career by destroying others; it is better to succeed in life on your own merits. If you wish to be successful, dedicate yourself to your work instead of putting others down in order to look better by comparison. Even your competitors should be treated honestly and fairly.

Daniel asked God for help and thus was able to reveal and interpret the king's dream. As a result, he received many rewards, but he wasn't selfish with them. He asked his friends to help him, and they were made managers of the business of the province.

Be careful: when you ask for an opportunity for someone else, make sure the person is capable and worthy of trust. Daniel recommended his friends because he knew they were competent and had integrity. Recommending someone without qualifications will not solve anyone's problem and may bring you headaches.

Integrity and Knowledge

Years later, under King Darius's reign, a management system was developed in which 120 representatives reported to three presidents. Daniel was one of the presidents and, since he proved to be the best, the king considered placing him at the top of the chain of command. Naturally this generated envy among the other officials: "The high officials and the satraps sought to find a ground for complaint against Daniel with regard to the kingdom, but they could find no ground for complaint or any fault, because he was faithful, and no error or fault was found in him" (Dan. 6:4 ESV).

The only solution his enemies thought of was to use Daniel's faith against him. If you have some type of faith or religion, prepare yourself, for this can be used as a pretext to harm you.

The conspiracy against Daniel went as planned. Daniel's adversaries convinced the king to sign a decree stating that no one could worship or petition another god or man except for King Darius under penalty of being thrown into the lions' den. Even knowing the consequences, Daniel remained committed to his values and, without attempting to hide it, continued to pray to his God.

The king was hurt by the condemnation of Daniel because he liked and admired him (after all, who doesn't like a good employee or manager?). Darius tried to find a way to save Daniel, but he came up against the immutability of his empire's laws. The prophet was thrown into the lions' den, and his regretful "boss" didn't sleep all night because of what he had been forced to do to his best "executive."

In the morning, King Darius went to the lions' den and called, "'Daniel, servant of the living God, has your God, whom you serve continually, been able to rescue you from the lions?' Daniel answered, 'May the king live forever! My God sent His angel, and He shut the mouths of the lions. They have not hurt me, because I was found innocent in His sight. Nor have I ever done any wrong before you, Your Majesty'" (Dan. 6:20–22).

Daniel had reason to be hurt and angry with the king, or even to criticize him or become arrogant for having survived the lions, but he treated the king with respect and kindness, thus demonstrating his character and wisdom. British essayist and thinker Samuel Johnson wrote, "Integrity without knowledge is weak and useless, and knowledge without integrity is dangerous and dreadful."[5] We should cultivate both of these virtues.

If someone hurts you or wrongs you, be gentle and magnanimous. Jesus says, "Love your enemies and pray for those who persecute you" (Matt. 5:44). Later in the Gospel of Matthew, we read, "Peter came up and said to Him, 'Lord, how often will my brother sin against me, and I forgive him? As many as seven times?' Jesus said to him, 'I do not say to you seven times, but seventy-seven times'" (18:21–22 ESV).

When Jesus was crucified, the apostle Peter denied him three times. After Jesus was resurrected, he sought out Peter and asked him three times if he loved him, to which Peter responded yes. Once again, Jesus gave Peter the mission of taking care of others and said, "Follow me!" (John 21:19).

Then Peter made another mistake, as we see in John 21:20–22 when he asked Jesus what would happen to the disciple Jesus loved who was now following them. Jesus answered, "If I want him to remain alive until I return, what is that to you? You must follow me" (v. 22). It is as if Jesus was saying, "That's not your problem, Peter. Take care of your own life and career, your own tasks, and don't worry about what I will do with others or what others are doing." Jesus gave Peter the mission of taking care of others, not of being in charge of them, monitoring them, or competing with them.

Perhaps the greatest difficulty in becoming a person of integrity is avoiding looking to the side and worrying about the fact that others don't act with the same level of loyalty and propriety. You shouldn't be a person of integrity as part of an exchange, in which your honesty will be proportional to the degree of honesty of those you interact with. Act with integrity without seeking recognition, award, or reward. Being a person of integrity depends on you and you alone. In his defense of integrity, Warren Buffett also said, "Honesty is a very expensive gift; don't expect it from cheap people."[6] Don't be a cheap person; in other words, give this expensive and rare gift to everyone.

The concept of Biblical integrity is clear: you should adopt it unconditionally. Note that the Ten Commandments teach that children should honor their parents whether they deserve it or not, spouses should honor their partners whether they deserve it or not, and employees should honor their bosses, and vice versa, whether they deserve it or not. These are based on the principle that God loves us whether we deserve it or not.

You cannot apply Biblical logic to the concept that "my good manners depend on yours." Sometimes maintaining a relationship depends on the conduct of another person, but ethics should not be relative. Ethics is not something that can be shaped according to the environment.

Let go of worrying about the behavior of others or expecting them to reciprocate. It is the principles *you* choose to follow that define your conduct; your principles are not determined by other people or by outside circumstances. This book is based on the certainty of the existence of the God who sees everything and has power over everything. He is the one who will reward us. Even if you don't share this level of certainty about God, act with integrity anyway and be patient. You will see results. Believing is seeing. Believe and act, and in so doing, you will see.

I am not a product of my circumstances.
I am a product of my decisions.
STEPHEN COVEY

TWELVE

The Law of
the Complete Set

Be diligent to present yourself approved to God
as a workman who does not need to be ashamed,
accurately handling the word of truth.

2 Timothy 2:15 NASB

The essential qualities that a professional should have to
guarantee their place in the job market were listed in the
Law of Entrepreneurship. As we have seen, you need to be
a hard worker, competent, honest, pleasant, loyal and reliable, determined and persistent, patient, humble, a team
player, and resilient. These are secular attributes that anyone
can develop, even those who do not have faith in God. But
the Law of the Complete Set possesses a strong spiritual

dimension that seeks higher objectives than professional or financial success.

The Law of the Complete Set has common traits with the Law of Integrity but goes a step beyond. It is not enough just to have character, to be honest, and to be worthy of trust. We need to develop a set of virtues that distinguish us as outstanding humans, above average even in spiritual terms. The Greek word for this is *teleios*, a word that means "complete."

God should be at the center of our everyday actions, as we saw in the Law of Maximum Quality. We should fulfill our duties—not only at work but also in other areas of our lives—as though we were serving God. According to Pastor Larry Titus in his book *The Teleios Man: Your Ultimate Identity*, reaching this stage is to be "complete, finished, perfection"[1]—in other words, reflecting the perfection of Christ in each part of our lives and serving as examples to others.

The Scripture passage that opens this chapter speaks of being "approved" and advises the worker or businessperson—the laborer—to "accurately [handle] the word of truth" (1 Tim. 2:15 NASB). This means not only knowing God's Word but also practicing it, which transforms us into *teleios*, people who reach a level of spirituality in which the fruit of the Holy Spirit is present.

Here is the complete set of the fruit of the Spirit as described in Galatians 5:22–23 (NASB):

• Love

• Joy

• Peace

• Patience

- Kindness
- Goodness
- Faithfulness
- Gentleness
- Self-control

We may not begin our journey with this complete set of extraordinary virtues, but we should attempt to develop them. To achieve this, we need God's intervention. Our divine partner is not concerned with investing in buildings or products but in people. His desire is to see us growing according to the skills He gave us. He is the shepherd, and we are the sheep. His aim is for us to be filled with the Holy Spirit, leading to internal results, which the Bible refers to as "fruit" (Gal. 5:22).

The external results are mere consequences of this internal spiritual transformation. It is important to highlight that the Law of the Complete Set does not have any direct relation to success or money. Those who try to follow it in order to obtain material wealth have not understood the gospel, the good news that Jesus brought to the world. Our motivation should be to become who God wants us to be. *

It is worth noting, however, that these spiritual qualities are appreciated by everyone, from family members to work relationships. Who wouldn't want to be with a loving, good, joyful, generous person who exudes faith and peace? Who wouldn't want to work alongside such a person, have such a partner, buy a product from such an individual, or hire someone with these qualities? In this regard—not necessarily as an aim, but as a consequence—putting the Law of the

Complete Set into practice will have positive repercussions on your career and your finances.

We believe this complete set of virtues, especially faith, is something that can be obtained and perfected only with the help of the Holy Spirit. The idea of peace and joy in any circumstance only makes sense through the vision of the peace of Christ expressed in the Bible: "Peace I leave with you; my peace I give you. I do not give to you as the world gives. Do not let your hearts be troubled and do not be afraid" (John 14:27). We hope you will seek and find this peace. *for I have overcome the world. —Jesus*

Throughout the centuries there were men
who took first steps, down new roads, armed
with nothing but their own vision.

Ayn Rand

THIRTEEN

The Law of Generous Resiliency

Whenever you face trials of any kind, consider it nothing but joy, because you know that the testing of your faith produces endurance; and let endurance have its full effect, so that you may be mature and complete, lacking in nothing.

James 1:2–4 NRSV

Knowing how to face obstacles and resist adversity while still continuing to learn, help others, and do good are qualities that are exalted in the Bible. That is why there are various laws that deal with this theme, among them the Law of Resilience (described in *The 25 Biblical Laws of Success*), the Law of Training, and the Law of Well-Rewarded Affliction.

In all these laws, we see the importance of not giving up on our goals or changing who we are just because we are going through tough times.

The Law of Generous Resiliency is a mixture of this persistence with a strong component of generosity. The result is the capacity to suffer injustice without being contaminated by it.

It is a paradox that people who cultivate generous resiliency often face great challenges. The Bible warns us that precious metals are refined through fire. Solomon says in Proverbs 17:3: "The crucible for silver and the furnace for gold, but the LORD tests the heart." Precious metals are submitted to high temperatures in the melting pot (silver) and in the oven (gold) to remove impurities. Solomon said, "Remove the impurities from silver, and the sterling will be ready for the silversmith" (Prov. 25:4 NLT).

Even with their impurities, silver is silver and gold is gold. The goldsmith puts aside the good part and knows how to use it. God, the greatest goldsmith of all, performs the same task: He purifies our hearts through afflictions and trials, cleaning the silver and gold in order to forge us into precious vessels for His use.

If you are willing to have the dirt removed from your life, what will be left is precious metal that can be used and molded by God. Be careful about the people you associate with and don't forget the Law of the Company You Keep (described in *The 25 Biblical Laws of Success*). As the Portuguese proverb warns, "If you associate with hogs, be prepared to eat scraps." In any government or company, getting rid of bad leadership and the "bad apples" is essential for success: "Remove the wicked from the king's court, and his reign will be made secure by justice" (Prov. 25:5 NLT).

Everyone deserves a second chance, but when a person insists on remaining stagnant, the best you or your company can do is to give them the opportunity to grow somewhere else. Who knows, maybe by losing their job they will recognize their mistakes, improve their behavior, and increase productivity. Recognize your limits: if you have tried but have not been able to get the best out of your subordinates, give them a chance with another boss or leader.

The Paradox of the Good Professional

Have you ever noticed that more is required of the best employees and the best public servants while the lazy ones just loaf around? This is where we apply the laws of partnership with God that we have been studying.

Contrary to what seems right, the best projects suffer most. The most revolutionary ideas are precisely the ones that encounter the most opposition. The best men and women will be the ones to face the greatest challenges.

It is naive to believe that the best people will be spared suffering and that only the wicked will have to endure trials. While we know that everyone reaps what they sow and, therefore, the wicked will go through bad times, we have to admit, reluctantly, that the good also suffer. The Bible, as we have seen, says that the more precious a metal is, the more will be required of it. Bad metal is tossed aside.

106

The same happens with clay. It is transformed only in the hands of the potter. In order to become something of value, it must first be shaped. The clay will continue to be clay; it will remain clay in its essence. Yet the potter, or God, will give it a more noble form and purpose. And the clay, like gold, only reaches its potential after spending hours in the oven.

The precious metal that does not become a piece of jewelry and the clay that does not become a sculpture, vase, tile, or brick may not have suffered, but it has failed to fulfill its full potential. If you are feeling the heat of the oven and sense ~~that~~ much is required of you, it is most likely because you are valuable clay or a precious metal. Rest assured ~~that~~ if you remain firm and let yourself be purified of the impurities within, you will be transformed into something useful and beautiful——as much for yourself as for the world.

Job's Trials

There are many successful men and women in the Bible, such as Joseph, Caleb, Samuel, Jabez, Esther, and Gideon. There are also various characters who could be taken as examples of either success or failure, such as Samson, Saul, and David. We can learn from all of them, primarily from those who made a lot of mistakes, such as Rachel, Jonah, Ananias, and Sapphira. To some degree, all these men and women demonstrated resilience, but not always in a joyful or generous way. We find an excellent example of generous resiliency in the story of Job.

His case is compelling. Job was a man of great integrity, father to seven sons and three daughters, and very wealthy.

Everything in his life was going well until a certain day when Satan approached the Lord. The two talked, and the Lord asked Satan, "Have you considered my servant Job? There is no one on earth like him; he is blameless and upright, a man who fears God and shuns evil" (Job 1:8). Satan responded that it was easy for Job to be that way since he was blessed by God. He proposed a test: "But now stretch out your hand and strike everything he has, and he will surely curse you to your face" (v. 11).

To prove Job's integrity, God permitted Satan to interfere in his life. What resulted was a true tragedy: Job lost his property, his wealth, and his children, and he was left suffering, his body covered in boil-like sores. Despite this, he did not blaspheme God. On the contrary, he declared, "Naked I came from my mother's womb, and naked I will depart. The LORD gave and the LORD has taken away; may the name of the LORD be praised" (v. 21).

Hearing of his suffering, three of Job's friends went to comfort him, and they began to debate the magnitude of divine purposes and the mysteries of life. In the end, God appeared and reprimanded Job's friends, warning that He would punish them unless Job said a prayer for them. After praying for his friends, Job received from the Lord twice as much as he had before. The Lord blessed him with seven more sons and three more daughters, and Job lived a long and prosperous life.

From a careful reading of the book of Job, we can extract many qualities that we may strive to develop:

- Job was upright and just, <u>fearing</u> God and avoiding evil.
- He was concerned for his children, and everything indicates ~~that~~ he was <u>faithful</u> in his marriage.
- He was a source of pride in the eyes of his superior (in this case, God) and fair with his employees.
- He dealt with setbacks and tragedies with humble resignation.
- He resisted even family pressure in order to maintain his integrity.
- He was not obsessed with money or wealth.
- He did not rejoice in other peoples' sufferings.
- He admitted his mistakes and was transparent.

Job endured <u>all</u> these difficulties and then recovered, rebuilt his business, and started a new family. His example shows ~~that~~, even after terrible disasters, it is possible to start a new life, especially if you have a strong emotional framework and if your success is established on a solid foundation.

Finding things for which one can be grateful helps make the memory of a difficult experience less intrusive. Other research has found a connection between the kind of positive emotions created by gratitude and resilience. Grateful people are better able to weather life's storms.

DEBORAH NORVILLE

109

FOURTEEN

The Law of the Ten Steps

Those who do what is right come to the light
so others can see ~~that~~ they are doing what God
wants.

John 3:21 NLT

The Ten Commandments are a great set of rules, but unfortunately they are often perceived as a set of prohibitions, a disagreeable list of what we can't do. Yet these ten rules represent a fantastic manual ~~that~~, if put into practice, will make you an outstanding person in many areas.

Besides <u>teaching</u> important values for relationships and spiritual life, the Ten Commandments indicate how to achieve success, prosperity, and personal growth. Whether out of religious devotion or a desire to improve your techniques for success, you will have great results if you follow the Law of the Ten Steps. In <u>practice</u>, this is not just one law,

but ten! Yet ten steps are not many for someone who truly
~~wishes~~ desires to become a partner with God.

During the growth process, there is a place for pruning—
and these cuts, when done properly, refine rather than damage. As Brazilian writer Cecília Meireles said, "I learned
from the Springs to allow myself to be cut so I could come
back whole."[1] We believe ~~that~~ by respecting the limits imposed by the Ten Commandments, we can become emotionally and spiritually whole.

Consider what each of the commandments teaches:

1. *"You shall have no other gods before me"* (Exod.
   20:3). Atheists, skeptics, and materialists—not only
   religious people—can learn a lot from this advice.
   How? Work and money can become like gods in the
   lives of many people. And those who deify these
   things become workaholics. If you are going to follow any god, follow the real One.

2. *"You shall not make for yourself an image in the
   form of anything in heaven above or on the earth
   beneath or in the waters below"* (v. 4). The true God
   is infinite; He doesn't fit in a drawing or an image. He
   manifests Himself through nature, people, the Bible,
   and even silence. God is a Spirit, and we should learn
   not to try to materialize Him. Trust God, especially
   during adversity.

3. *"You shall not misuse the name of the LORD your
   God"* (v. 7). Be known for your own word, without

111

having to use the name of God. Those who use the name of the Lord to gain trust do so because they have not been able to gain trust on their own.

4. *"Remember the Sabbath day by keeping it holy"* (v. 8). Regardless of religious faith, we advise people to rest on the Sabbath day. Resting one day each week reduces illness, strengthens the emotional state, and increases productivity. It works for those who are studying for competitive exams as well as those who are starting a business. It is valid for any type of activity. It is vital that you take a day of rest, which, for most people, takes place on Sunday. In professional terms, more important than the actual day of the week is the concept of having a day of rest and leisure.

5. *"Honor your father and your mother, so that you may live long in the land the LORD your God is giving you"* (v. 12). You can't choose the type of parents you will have, but you can choose the type of child you will be. This type of loving discipline can change your family history: by being a good child, you are preparing to be a good parent. By not responding in kind but turning the other cheek, as Jesus commanded in Matthew 5:39, you can become an exceptional person and one in whom God takes pleasure. If you believe in the God who loves you unconditionally, in spite of your flaws, you should learn to love others in the same way. Start acting like this with

your parents and your children, and then try to do the same with work colleagues, bosses, or subordinates. Love isn't just what you feel; love is also what you do.

6. *"You shall not murder"* (v. 13). Preserving life, yours and others', will benefit your body, your mind, those who live around you, and the planet.

7. *"You shall not commit adultery"* (v. 14). Moral judgments aside, those who commit adultery lose focus and energy. Certainly, it will take much effort to keep an extramarital affair hidden and to manage two relationships. The waste of emotional energy and time will reflect in your work.

8. *"You shall not steal"* (v. 15). Those who steal can lose their jobs (on justifiable grounds) and may be criminally prosecuted. We could add the following to this commandment: "and you shall not commit fraud."

9. *"You shall not give false testimony against your neighbor"* (v. 16). This rule warns of the damage that gossip and intrigue cause in a work environment. Slander creates terrible results in a company's operation, in public service, and even in your own business. Jesus taught, "Bless those who curse you, pray for those who mistreat you" (Luke 6:28). This may seem contradictory, but those who ignore provocation and refuse to waste time and energy on conflicts often come out stronger in the end. If what is said about

113

someone is not true or relevant, everyone will perceive the ill intent of the person who speaks badly of another.

10. *"You shall not covet your neighbor's house. You shall not covet your neighbor's wife, or his male or female servant, his ox or donkey, or anything that belongs to your neighbor"* (v. 17). If you want something ~~that~~ you don't have, then strive for it honestly. Don't focus on what isn't yours; instead, work to earn what you would like. Coveting will not bring you any benefits, only frustration. Envy and jealousy are negative feelings that cause you to waste energy on unhealthy thoughts. When trying to be like others, you fail to focus on your own talents. In other words, it is the jealous person who loses out. This piece of divine advice is saying, "Go live your life, and stop living the lives of others."

A New Way of Looking at the Ten Commandments

Instead of viewing the Ten Commandments as prohibitions, we should see them as challenges and guideposts to improve our lives.[2] How do artists transform a piece of marble or wood into a sculpture? They remove from the raw material everything that doesn't match up to the sculpture they envision. If they want to make a wooden horse, they chisel off pieces of wood not needed to form a horse. What is left will be something that resembles the animal the sculptor ~~wished~~ *desired* to create.

So it is with the Ten Commandments. They were given to remove from people the imperfections that make us defeated, delinquent, unsocial, immoral, hateful, slovenly, reckless, dishonorable, envious, resentful, and so on. What is left, then, is a "more perfect" human being.

The Ten Commandments are not the rules of an obstinate and authoritative deity, ready to take away all joy from his followers; God wouldn't have gone to the trouble simply to populate the planet with sad people. In giving the Ten Commandments to Moses, God shows love for his creation. It doesn't make sense for the Creator to liberate people only to then have them submit to a series of rules everyone feels tempted to disrespect.

More than commands, these ten steps are words of encouragement, motivation, hope, and faith. It is from this perspective that we should look at the Ten Commandments. They are challenges that will help us mature emotionally. Where there is no challenge, there is simply stagnation and monotony. And still water becomes unsanitary.

Consider the opportunities offered by the Ten Commandments to overcome challenges in the following examples. These practices may not always be easy, but they will be worth it.

"Remember the Sabbath day by keeping it holy" (Exod. 20:8). Manage your time well, which is one of the great secrets of success. Get organized so that you don't have to think about work at least one day of every seven. Practice creative leisure, and use this break in your routine as an opportunity to expand your horizons and cultivate new ideas.

"You shall not murder" (v. 13). Respect all life, which includes not killing yourself little by little due to an excess of work or a disregard of your physical and emotional needs. Don't kill off the expressions of your own personality or those of others, such as self-esteem and respectability; these too are projections of the idea of respecting life.

"You shall not commit adultery" (v. 14). Create a fulfilling relationship with your spouse, which will result in savings (of time and money) and fewer risks (of injury, diseases, sorrows, and separation). It will also allow you to reach deeper levels of intimacy, pleasure, and maturity with your loved one, since you are fully investing in that relationship.

"You shall not steal" (v. 15). Create wealth through work, not by cheating others. Even if you are not caught taking something that isn't yours, by stealing you will become increasingly impoverished. A theft might bring you some material advantage, but morally you will lose more and more value.

"You shall not give false testimony against your neighbor" (v. 16). Speak the truth, play fair, and be honest with yourself and others. This will ensure that your word has value, and it will give you credibility with others.

"You shall not covet your neighbor's house. You shall not covet your neighbor's wife, or his male or female servant, his ox or donkey, or anything that belongs to your neighbor" (v. 17). On the one hand, strive to be content with what you have. It is very gratifying to live by this philosophy. And if you wish to have more, then work to achieve your goals. On the

desire

other hand, <u>learn</u> to be happy for the achievements of others. ✓
Accept ~~that~~ God gives good things to everyone.

In summary, there are many obstacles ~~that~~, if overcome,
will change you into an extraordinary person in <u>all</u> areas of
your life.

If you treat an individual as he is, he will
remain how he is. But if you treat him as if he
were what he ought to be and could be, he will
become what he ought to be and could be.

GOETHE

FIFTEEN

The Law of Helping Others

Anyone who loves God must also love their brother
and sister.

1 John 4:21

We are making good progress in the qualities that a legitimate partner of God needs to develop, and one of them is
the ability to help your neighbor through service. Ideally
you would do this willingly and not out of self-interest, but
either way, you will be rewarded.

In *The 25 Biblical Laws of Success*, we discussed the Law
of Usefulness, in which you become useful to others and
the company you work for, and as a result you receive more
professional recognition. The Law of Helping Others goes
beyond that: to help your neighbor because this is what Jesus
wants you to do. Even if you are not compensated for your
work, your attitude will be rewarded.

God acts in many ways, and He wants us to do the same in relation to others, motivated by His example of love and service. As you establish your priorities, don't simply focus on yourself. Follow the divine principles for building a better and more just world for everyone. It is good to remember that the "religion that God our Father accepts as pure and faultless is this: to look after orphans and widows in their distress and to keep oneself from being polluted by the world" (James 1:27).

Our all-powerful, divine partner is looking for associates who want to *give* rather than receive. Jesus is our ultimate example of the Law of Helping Others. He was born, He lived, and He died out of love for each one of us. If you believe this, then consider following this standard for an abundant life of service to others.

Even though one of our objectives is to grow professionally and improve our lives, we stress that Jesus said we should not try to "serve two masters" at the same time (Matt. 6:24). You cannot have both God and wealth as your masters. You must choose one or the other and focus on your priority. If you want to have a thriving partnership with God, you should establish God as your priority.

Happiness is not directly related to professional or financial successes and failures. We see the proof of this in the many rich and famous people who are often dissatisfied, as well as the many simple, ordinary people who seem to live in peace. Happiness stems from a set of attitudes, thoughts, and behaviors. In light of this, our circumstances become secondary.

119

The Bible teaches that God offers special help to those who reach out to others: "Oh, the joys of those who are kind to the poor! The LORD rescues them when they are in trouble" (Ps. 41:1 NLT). It is like a father who says to his son, "Help your brothers, and I will reward you for it." God wants us to concern ourselves with the poor and the needy and with those who are unjustly treated, persecuted, and discriminated against. His intent is that our love, attention, and education would be focused on helping others, including our enemies.

Those who reach this level of empathy with others are certainly people everyone wants to be with, talk to, and do business with. Of course, this should not be the reason for being good, but who wouldn't want to hire or do business with someone like that?

Take Care of Others, and God Will Take Care of Your Career

We are absolutely convinced that when you focus your attention on doing good and helping others, God takes care of your career. It is as if God helps you so that you can concentrate on what He considers to be most important: people. When you start focusing more on your career, God sees that you believe you are more capable of taking care of things than He is, and He respectfully intervenes less in your professional and financial path.

Beyond what God can do for you, remember that people appreciate those who care about them. Those who help others will be partners or professionals whom others want to have around. When you do good, you receive good in return, as we can see in many scriptural examples. Job prayed for his friends, and God restored what had been taken (Job 42:10). Esther risked her life for her people, and God saved her (the book of Esther). Mordecai took care of his people, and he was held in high esteem (Esther 10:3).

Caring for others will bring two types of consequences. On a strategic level, the more you are loved, the easier it is to become a leader and influence your group and to count on your team's motivation, loyalty, and commitment. Doing good works for others will bring you their admiration and gratitude. On a spiritual level, when you help others, God will be pleased with you and will bless your life in a special way: "Ship your grain across the sea; after many days you may receive a return" (Eccles. 11:1).

Rewarded Help versus Disinterested Help

It is good to remember that there is more than one way to view success. Some viewpoints—in which money, fame, and power have no importance—are completely foreign to most people. We are talking about individuals who dedicate themselves to serving God and others.

In this level of service, people are willing to sacrifice part of their time and assets in order to be useful to others. This usually occurs for greater motivations, either philanthropic or spiritual, which far exceed the professional realm.

Sometimes people choose to help others as a way to serve Christ. We know people who could have a far greater financial return on private projects but who choose instead to dedicate themselves to social work or missions. In this case, they are sacrificing some material possessions or a career to fulfill a goal that is more important to them.

The gospel has a wonderful aspect, that of salvation. It can also include another aspect that is also good, that of prosperity and wealth. Some choose the altruistic path of Jesus: "We know love by this, that He laid down His life for us—and we ought to lay down our lives for one another" (1 John 3:16 NRSV). Every time we are able to give life by donating and building, every time we prevent death, robbery, and destruction, we are participating in the work that Jesus said He came to do.

The plan for a life of love, righteousness, and service is clearly expressed in the message God gave to His people through His prophet Isaiah:

> Then you will call, and the LORD will answer;
> you will cry for help, and He will say: Here am I.
> If you do away with the yoke of oppression,
> with the pointing finger and malicious talk,
> and if you spend yourselves in behalf of the hungry
> and satisfy the needs of the oppressed,
> then your light will rise in the darkness,
> and your night will become like the noonday.
> The LORD will guide you always;
> He will satisfy your needs in a sun-scorched land
> and will strengthen your frame.
> You will be like a well-watered garden,
> like a spring whose waters never fail.
> (Isa. 58:9–11)

The amount of service you are willing to render to others depends only on you, but don't forget that loving your neighbor is one of the main clauses in your partnership with God.

Helping Your Neighbor and Servant Leadership

When we discuss the subject of leadership, most people think about rewards and status. Actually, while leadership is a high-profile job, it is also laborious and stressful, and it involves responsibilities, difficulties, and a lot of dedication. Taking on or accepting leadership of a group can be the fruit of a commitment to the Law of Helping Others.

If you help others, you will be more prepared to accept the charge of becoming a leader, and this will further develop your abilities. Be prepared to serve your subordinates, paying attention to what they say and showing them that they can count on you.

Rubens Teixeira, author of *How to Succeed When You're Not the Favorite*, has become a reference in regard to this aspect of leadership—serving others. Consider what he has to say about it: "Being proactive in helping can seem unimportant; however, for those who know how to discern the personal value of someone, a generous attitude is worth a lot, as it reveals sensibility and a capacity to serve. In some highly relevant activities of the society, only those with this profile have the means to perform well. Those who are not interested in others will certainly not be an engaged leader, capable of guiding others to producing good results and giving the best of themselves."[1]

In the same vein, Saint Francis of Assisi said:

> Lord, make me an instrument of Your peace:
> where there is hatred, let me sow love;
> where there is injury, pardon;
> where there is doubt, faith;
> where there is despair, hope;
> where there is darkness, light;
> and where there is sadness, joy.
>
> O divine Master, grant that I may not so much seek
> to be consoled as to console,
> to be understood as to understand,
> to be loved as to love.
> For it is in giving that we receive,
> it is in pardoning that we are pardoned,
> and it is in dying that we are born to eternal life.[2]

Thus, if you want to lead well, a good way to do it is for you to help others while you let God take care of your career.

The worth of a human being lies in the ability
to extend oneself, to go outside oneself,
to exist in and for other people.
MILAN KUNDERA

PART 4

Laws
concerning
Relationship
with God

SIXTEEN

The Law of Dependence

I am poor and needy; may the Lord think of me.
You are my help and my deliverer; You are my
God, do not delay.

Psalm 40:17

In four of the psalms he wrote, David repeated the phrase "I am poor and needy," even though he was a king, powerful and invincible in military and political might. David realized that in regard to the more serious subjects of life, we are all "poor and needy."

Jesus spoke of the same matter: "God blesses those who are poor and realize their need for Him, for the Kingdom of Heaven is theirs" (Matt. 5:3 NLT). What did He mean by this? Jesus was saying that those who perceive their own poverty or need can experience God's help. To understand this better, we can draw a parallel to those who are sick but see themselves as healthy and hence do not seek help. These people have less of a chance of being made well than those who recognize they are sick and seek medical aid.

Even though God's presence is constant in the world, those who actively seek God's help will receive it in a special way. David portrayed this dependence; he recognized his needs and took his requests to God. For example, he prayed, "See if there is any offensive way in me, and lead me in the way everlasting" (Ps. 139:24).

Many people, especially the rich and powerful, make the mistake of believing they don't depend on God for anything. This is why Jesus said, "It is easier for a camel to go through the eye of a needle than for a rich person to enter the Kingdom of God!" (Luke 18:25 NLT). It is worth clarifying that what hinders these people from entering heaven is not their possession of goods and wealth but rather their lack of faith and their arrogant and self-sufficient attitude.

David and Goliath

The fact that we are dependent on God doesn't mean that we don't have dreams and ambitions or that we stop fighting for what we want. By analyzing David's journey, we understand why he became a paragon of action and courage. As a youth, David was ambitious and had plans to grow and succeed. He didn't hide from anyone the fact that he was interested in the rewards promised to the person who could win the greatest challenge of his time: defeating the giant Goliath.

David determined to face Goliath since none of the soldiers of the army of Israel, not even the most prepared, were brave enough to do so. After arriving on the battlefield, he had asked those around him, "What will a man get for killing this Philistine and ending his defiance of Israel?" (1 Sam. 17:26 NLT). David had <u>faith</u> in God and was victorious. Therefore, it is important to emphasize that the Bible does not condemn positive ambitions; rather, it rebukes selfish ✳ ambition.

Though many people know the story of David and Goliath, few know that before young David went face-to-face with the giant, he had trained a lot. As a shepherd, David had already faced a lion and a bear (vv. 34–37). When wild animals attacked his flock, David could have run away and come up with excuses, saying, "A lion and a bear came to attack the flock, and I had to get away fast and leave the sheep there!" But he stayed and fought the predators. He didn't run away from the challenges that appeared, and this ✳ prepared him for even greater difficulties.

David was a teenager when he beat the giant Goliath. It is interesting that he admitted his limitations and still went to battle. He didn't try to pretend he was something he wasn't. When King Saul offered his armor, sword, and bronze helmet, David tried them on, but he didn't feel at ease using them and preferred to go to battle with his staff, slingshot, and five stones (vv. 38–40). There are many people who pretend to have knowledge or try to be someone they are not. Unfortunately, these people usually don't progress.

David didn't care about the taunts of his enemies or the people who bet he wouldn't win, preferring to <u>believe</u> in himself and in God. That is when the Law of <u>Faith</u> came into play. When the giant roared sarcastically "Am I a dog, . . . that you come at me with a stick?" David answered, "You come to me with sword, spear, and javelin, but I come to you in the name of the LORD of Heaven's Armies—the God of the armies of Israel, whom you have defied" (vv. 43, 45 NLT). <u>Faith</u> is capable of overcoming <u>fear</u>, insecurity, uncertainty, humiliation, weakness, and all the weapons meant to intimidate us.

✻ David demonstrated several characteristics of successful people: he <u>made plans</u>, <u>he trained</u>, he <u>was courageous</u>, he <u>perceived his limitations</u>, he <u>wasn't affected by criticism</u>, and he <u>fought with faith</u>. He proved to be a great leader, a courageous warrior, and, for those who <u>believe</u> in God, an example of <u>faith</u>. He is considered a "man after [God's] own heart" (Acts 13:22). His inspiring psalms are real lessons in how to commit to our goals.

But David also made mistakes—many of them. Nevertheless, his story shows us that, despite our flaws, we can still do good things. We can repent and get back on the right path.

It is worth mentioning that David erred when he began to get too confident in himself and stopped going to battle with his army. When King David became too comfortable in his palace, he saw and coveted Bathsheba, Uriah's wife. To make matters worse, he began to <u>believe</u> he had more rights than others and thus committed adultery. Then, to hide his mistake, he committed murder, betraying and killing one of his most faithful soldiers by sending him to the most dangerous place on the battlefield. This mistake cost him dearly. But David didn't lose his faith, and God forgave him.

Notice what Jesus tells us about the Law of Dependence: "I am the vine; you are the branches. If you remain in me and I in you, you will bear much fruit; apart from me you can do nothing" (John 15:5).

I have held many things in my hands, and I
have lost them all; but whatever I have placed
in God's hands, that I still possess.

Martin Luther

131

SEVENTEEN

The Law of Patience

I waited patiently for the LORD; He inclined to
me and heard my cry.

Psalm 40:1 NRSV

Patience is an essential tool for dealing with obstacles and
with the time between our actions (sowing) and the intended
results (harvest). Patience is the calmness we need to wait
for what may be slow in coming, and it involves standing by
for a change of scene.

Perseverance is a virtue, but patience goes beyond it, for
patience involves trust in divine provision. It is one thing
to persist in a dream or project; it's another thing to wait
patiently for the Lord.

We should not want to take over God's part or be in a
hurry for Him to act according to our plans. Nor should we
try to accelerate things by breaking rules, especially those

132

ordained by God. Being in God's service doesn't give anyone the right to disregard either Biblical laws or human laws.

Honesty, for example, is essential for true success. God doesn't need anyone to give him a little extra help by using illicit or unethical methods. This is one of the worst distortions that occur on the way to success. It is regrettable, but there are people who believe that the ends justify the means and that it doesn't hurt to be dishonest, commit petty thefts or fraud, participate in corruption, cheat on taxes, or be involved in shady deals. This kind of conduct may work sometimes, but there will be punishment, especially for those who claim to believe in God.

You have probably heard the story of Sarah, Abraham's wife, as told in the book of Genesis. God had promised that Sarah would have a child in her old age, but due to her impatience, she decided to take matters into her own hands. She gave her maid, Hagar, to Abraham, and Ishmael was born from this union. Years later, however, when Sarah was very old, God did bless Sarah with a son, Isaac, and from him a great nation was formed.

God had big plans for Sarah and Abraham, but their impatience led them to try to resolve their problems on their own, generating complications even today. Jews and Arabs are all descendants of Abraham—Jews from Isaac and Arabs from Ishmael—but they do not get along. Note that though Abraham and Sarah failed miserably, God still kept His promise. ✓

Another example of inappropriate haste is that of King Saul, whose story is told in the book of 1 Samuel. King Saul disobeyed God on more than one occasion. One of his mistakes was not waiting seven days for the arrival of the prophet Samuel, as was arranged, and taking upon himself actions that were for the priest of Israel alone—presiding over the sacrifices. Ironically, as soon as Saul completed the burnt offering, the prophet Samuel arrived, still within the arranged time.

To make matters worse, Saul did not repent of his disobedience; instead, he made excuses, such as it was an emergency, his people were dispersing, and the Philistines could attack at any moment. In extreme situations like this, God tests our faith. Contrary to what Saul presumed, we can't overlook the rules just because disaster seems imminent. Saul believed he could change the order of things just a little bit and God would understand. But God does not condone these detours.

On another occasion, Saul felt insecure and afraid. He had asked for God's help, but when he didn't get an immediate response, he allowed himself to be overtaken by distress. He disguised himself and consulted a necromancer and tried to speak to the dead. But he became even more desperate than before, which was the fruit of his haste. When someone ✳ makes a mistake, there is no use trying to hide from God. The Bible teaches that God is omniscient (He knows all things) and omnipresent (He is everywhere at once).

From the moment you make an agreement with God, accepting His intervention, you will receive not only benefits but also responsibilities. After putting yourself under God's authority, you have a Father. And any good father educates his ✳ children through discipline. Those who think it isn't worth submitting to this discipline do not realize ~~that~~ the Father who does the educating is the One who does the blessing. ✓ Until you submit to God, this may not be evident, but it will become clearer as you mature in your spiritual journey.

Acting out of impatience and "playing dirty" are always bad choices. They can destroy your reputation and drive away potential clients, suppliers, or partners.

Learn to wait. If, after all your effort and determination, you are still not seeing results, be patient. Between acceptance and anxiety, choose acceptance.

REBBE NACHMAN OF BRESLOV

EIGHTEEN

The Law of
Stewardship

Give an account of your stewardship.

Luke 16:2 NKJV

One of the most radical concepts of the Bible is this: you are *
not the real owner of what you have! You are just a steward,
a manager, someone who must give an account for what is
under your responsibility. The Law of Stewardship will make
you more zealous and less pretentious, recognizing that it is
God who gave you what you possess and that your obligation is to care for what He has given you and to be thankful *
for it. If this perspective scares you, think of it in terms of
share control: God has at least 51 percent of the shares of *no He*
everything that is yours. *has 100%*

136

What would happen if God had the controlling share of your business? Or if He were the mentor of your career? And what if you, an industrialist, the president of a company, or a manager or owner of a small business, considered everything you possess—goods, status, abilities, and influence—as belonging to God and not to you?

Think about it. Shouldn't someone who wants to follow Jesus and who has already offered his or her life to Him also put all their belongings at His disposal? After all, isn't life more important than material things? It doesn't make sense to give God what we have of greatest value (ourselves) and not give Him what we have of lesser value (our assets).

By following the twenty-five biblical laws of success, we can all obtain goods and wealth. According to the Law of Stewardship, however, we understand that it is God Who gives us everything we have; we could not acquire these things on our own. So we should share our success and help others, following a policy of healthy management about what we own: "Do not trust in oppression and do not vainly hope in robbery; if riches increase, do not set your heart upon them" (Ps. 62:10 NASB).

If you behave as a steward of God's resources, you will manage your possessions and how you treat others with greater responsibility. When politicians, judges, and business owners follow this principle, they are better people and less apt to commit abuse. The Law of Stewardship reminds us of the modern views of inquiry and accountability (being accountable to others and to yourself), procedures that are increasingly valued in society and in business.

Stewardship versus Leadership

Relationships that involve some type of subordination or authority can lead to the incorrect impression that we somehow "own" people. Parents can <u>believe</u> they own their children, spouses can think of their mates as their property, and bosses and leaders (religious, civilian, and military) can consider themselves owners of their employees. This is absurd. The Law of Stewardship helps put an end to the idea of possession, preventing disrespect, mistreatment, and criminal conduct, such as slave labor. We are not anyone's owner; we simply have the privilege of living and working with some people for a while. This understanding can transform the way we relate to others.

When dealing with employees or less experienced associates, we should act as if our divine partner has placed them under our tutelage. This applies to family members as well. If we act according to this idea, we will be considerate without being possessive. We shouldn't try to hold on to people. We should motivate them to grow and develop themselves, even if that means taking a different path than ours.

In his interview "Leader to Leader," Jack Welch affirmed that one of the characteristics of a great leader is to allow the people being led to grow. He stated that many bosses choose not to recommend their subordinates for higher-level positions or promotions so that they won't run the risk of losing these employees from their own teams. Good leaders, however, have the foresight and generosity to open doors for those who they <u>believe</u> deserve these <u>opportunities</u>, even though their own team may at first be shorthanded. In the long run, these bosses will have a greater capacity to attract new talents.[1]

As leaders, we can apply the lessons ~~that~~ Kahlil Gibran bequeathed us in his essay, "On Children," from the book *The Prophet*. It is about children but can easily be adapted to those working under you or to younger or less experienced people.

Your children are not your children.
They are the sons and daughters of Life's longing for itself.
They come through you but not from you,
And though they are with you, yet they belong not to you.
You may give them your love but not your thoughts.
For they have their own thoughts.
You may house their bodies but not their souls,
For their souls dwell in the house of tomorrow, which you cannot visit, not even in your dreams.
You may strive to be like them, but seek not to make them like you.
For life goes not backward nor tarries with yesterday.
You are the bows from which your children as living arrows are sent forth.
The archer sees the mark upon the path of the infinite, and He bends you with His might that His arrows may go swift and far.
Let your bending in the Archer's hand be for gladness;
For even as He loves the arrow that flies, so He loves also the bow that is stable.[2]

In conclusion, the idea of stewardship—managing, not owning—prepares us for the most difficult aspect of human reality: death. Knowing that we will not always have those we love close to us gives us a greater sense of love, service, and also urgency.

We need to free ourselves from consumerism.
Learn to say "no" to false needs and superfluous
purchases: you will have won a small battle against
yourself and you will still be free of numerous
problems. We must resist the seductions of the
consumer society and the worship of money: our
satisfaction must be in the Lord. God is our joy.
WILLIAM DOUGLAS AND DAVI LAGO

NINETEEN

The Law of Worship

In everything give thanks; for this is the will of
God in Christ Jesus for you.

1 Thessalonians 5:18 NKJV

Gratitude is a rare virtue these days because people have lost the habit of giving thanks and are not afraid to be disloyal to their friends, colleagues, and bosses. Being grateful to other human beings is the basis of the Law of Gratitude, which we covered in our previous book, *The 25 Biblical Laws of Success*. But in this book, the Law of Worship deals specifically with gratitude directed to God—and since it is directed toward the Father, it is on a higher dimension and has the character of worship.

Being grateful to God is an admirable quality because it makes us humble and less subject to arrogance. It is worth noting that in general an excess of self-confidence causes people to make mistakes. That is how the *Titanic*, considered at the time to be unsinkable, hit an iceberg and went down during its maiden voyage.

The Law of Worship is about our human ability to give thanks to God for our success, as we see in the Old Testament: "Otherwise, you may say in your heart, 'My power and the strength of my hand made me this wealth.' But you shall remember the LORD your God, for it is He who is giving you power to make wealth, that He may confirm His covenant which He swore to your fathers, as it is this day" (Deut. 8:17–18 NASB).

Always give God the credit for giving you the strength to get what you desire. If you would rather not put God's intervention in the picture, then at least try to abolish your self-sufficiency. Don't assume that the power and might of your hand is what will give you power. The wise Solomon declared, "Trust in the LORD with all your heart and lean not on your own understanding" (Prov. 3:5).

Many people claim to be thankful to God for all that they have, and that is commendable, but others transform this sentiment of worship into something more practical and effective. We shouldn't just recognize God's guidance in our lives; we should also maintain a spirit of humility and acknowledgment. This requires being content and thankful to God, regardless of the circumstances, and giving Him all the glory for our success.

We can worship God in many ways—not just in church services with songs of praise, sermons, offerings, and tithes. We can praise God in everything we do, whether we are sweeping the floor, cooking a meal, taking care of our children, work-ing hard, providing outstanding service, or creating a good product.

The Law of Worship can help us to break paradigms. We know that many people attribute their success to their own abilities. Others may recognize the help of third par-ties, but deep down they are still glorifying themselves. One way to change this self-centered view is to recognize God's intervention in our achievements—after all, without Him, we wouldn't even be alive. The next step is to transform our lives and work into a form of worship by using our abilities to contribute to social justice and to help others. As the Bible says, "In the same way, let your light shine before others, that they may see your good deeds and glorify your Father in heaven" (Matt. 5:16). Be brilliant not for yourself but for God.

We are entering radical territory, one in which people don't care if they win or lose or whether they are successful. For them, what matters is honoring God. This perspective is little known in the secular world and even in churches, but it reinforces all the other concepts and strengthens the meaning of our work lives.

The film *Facing the Giants* illustrates this concept.[1] This movie tells the story of Grant Taylor, a Christian high school football coach who was discredited and who felt dejected about never having had a winning season. Then a mysterious intervention changed his destiny and that of his team. From then on, the players were no longer worried about winning but about glorifying God. If we face our work every day as

143

if it were service to God, then any success we experience
would be a mere consequence. The liberating potential of
this attitude is amazing.

Those who wish to be instruments in God's hands do their
part, regardless of what they will achieve. Work is transformed into a vehicle of blessings to others. God wants to
bless people, and in this endeavor, He wants us as partners.
And it is precisely at this point that we can reach the highest
level of success.

Not everyone will have this objective, but if you want to
pursue partnership with God, consider applying this law in
your life: make your job and your success a way of honoring God.

We are perishing for want of wonder,
not for want of wonders.

G. K. CHESTERTON

TWENTY

The Law of Submission

Seek <u>first</u> His kingdom and His righteousness, and
<u>all</u> these things will be given to you as well.

Matthew 6:33

God's great enterprise on earth is to establish His kingdom—
the implementation of a new "company"—with <u>all</u> the challenges that come with it. Our priority, as His partners, is <u>first</u>
to take care of this endeavor, which He sees as more important than our careers or our businesses. This is the Law of
Submission.

As Pastor Rick Warren says in his book *The Purpose Driven
Life*, "It's not about you." As much as this clashes with our
vanity and individualism, Warren clearly explains: "The purpose of your life is far greater than your own personal fulfillment, your <u>peace</u> of mind, or even your happiness. It's far
greater than your family, your career, or even your wildest

dreams and ambitions. If you want to know why you were placed on this planet, you must begin with God. You were born by His purpose and for His purpose."[1]

Pastors Jeremias Pereira (senior pastor of 8th Presbyterian Church in Belo Horizonte, MG) and Ricardo Agreste (senior pastor of Chácara Primavera Presbyterian Church in Campinas, SP) both claim that God's commitment is not to produce happiness in us but maturity. Happiness doesn't produce maturity—we know a lot of people who say they are happy but are childish and immature. With maturity, however, it is possible to develop a healthy degree of happiness. In the end, as a result of a process of personal growth and maturity, both professional success and your own happiness will emerge. They are the fruit, not the tree.

If you look after the things of God, He will take care of your career. In fact, God will take care of both of your careers: the secular one and the spiritual one. The Law of Submission is another version of a principle that we covered in the Law of Helping Others: take care of people, and God will take care of your career. A reading of 1 Kings 6:38–7:1 reveals that first Solomon completed the construction of the house of God, and only then did he finish building his own house, a demonstration of how his priorities lined up: first the kingdom of God and then the rest.

While we are talking about priorities, it is worth mentioning this verse: "Do your planning and prepare your fields before building your house" (Prov. 24:27 NLT). Many people first want to buy a beautiful house and a great car, putting their investments in a solid financial foundation on the

back burner. This is foolish behavior. First, you build your
knowledge, then you build your company, and only then,
with security, do you make larger investments in your luxury
and comfort.

If you are not a Christian, your mission is to be happy,
achieve your dreams the best way you can, and strive to be
fulfilled. If you are a Christian, however, there are two levels
of living. There's the path in which you decide to live a righteous life before God, but you do not delve deeper into your
commitment to God's kingdom. If you choose this path,
you will be blessed; you will be a person of integrity and a
pillar within your society. But if you wish, you can take an
even more daring step—to make it your mission to be in
the center of God's will. Our dreams are important, and
Jesus wants us to have life in abundance (John 10:10), but
the expectation is that you ask yourself what mission God
has reserved for you.

One of the first biblical laws of success, described in our
previous book, is the Law of Vision. You need to have a clear
view of what you want out of life. What is your mission,
your dream, the reason you are here? In this book, once
again, the idea is to go beyond limitations. The Law of Submission involves, as its name suggests, submitting our personal mission and vision to the mission and vision God has
for us.

There are many ways of discovering God's vision for our
lives, and, generally speaking, we believe that God blesses
our dreams and desires (Ps. 37). Some people wish to be
business executives, presidents of companies, or celebrities,

but these goals should not be the focus of our relationship ✓
with God. In her DVD *The Spiritual Man and Discernment*,
Joyce Meyer deals appropriately with the idea of putting
God in the background:

> More is not always better. I am glad that everyone wants to
> grow, but first we need to be a blessing. Wanting more just
> to have more is not good. This is a consumer mind-set. We
> need to want more to bless more. ✳
>
> Many people want to be great preachers, famous musi-
> cians, ministers, and such. But few are called to that. Most ✳
> people are called to be common people. Do you know what
> your calling is? What everyone's calling is? What does God
> want you to do? The answer: wherever you happen to be,
> live a Christian life.[2] ✳

If you don't want a Christian life, that is your prerogative.
If you do, that is also your choice. You can choose where to
go; and wherever you are, you can live a Christian life. That
will be wonderful. If you desire, however, you can go beyond
and put yourself before God, submitting your life to Him, ✓
even if it means doing things you never imagined but that
He asks of you. The degree of surrender to God, whatever it
may be, should be done voluntarily and intentionally. ✳

If you want to ask God what He wants for your life, there ✓
will probably be an answer and you just need to follow it.
However, if there isn't an answer, or while you are waiting for
an answer, God wants you to make your choices, go where ✓
you feel is best, and *live a Christian life.*

In the following table, we see that there are different levels of commitment:

FIRST LEVEL	SECOND LEVEL	THIRD LEVEL
Gratitude	Gratitude to God	Worship
Usefulness	Helping others (for rewards)	Helping others (not interested in rewards)
Vision	Vision plus service to God	Vision submitted to the will of God

Gratitude: In the first level, you are grateful to people and to life. In the second level, you add thankfulness to God. In the third level, you finally arrive at the place where whatever you do is a form of worship.

Usefulness: In the first level, you are useful in order to achieve professional success with clients and work associates. In the second level, you try to be helpful to others in order to attain certain benefits, letting God take care of your career. In the third level, you are useful to everyone and to God out of love, being available for whatever task you can do to help others, without seeking rewards.

Vision: In the first level, you create a vision for your life and career. In the second level, you add to this vision some form of service to God. In the third level, you go beyond and submit your vision and personal mission to the filter of God's will, making God your priority.

If you choose the first level, great! You will already be above average. Not going to the next level doesn't mean that you are bad or a sinner or selfish. It is an option, and all options are valid and legitimate. If you choose the second level, you will be faced with another model of success, and you will be a person who is useful for God's purposes. Some decide to go even further and work to achieve the third level. One level does not exclude the others: each step or degree is a new and optional dimension with unique challenges and different results in your personal and professional life.

Diving into Faith

Complete submission to God is only attained when a person accepts being filled by the Spirit, like a cup that is filled with water, or even better, like a cup that overflows with the water of life.

There are several levels of submission to God, and we can draw a parallel to the levels of difficulty the man faced as he tried to cross rising waters, as narrated in the vision of Ezekiel 47:1–6.

The easiest phase, as if you are walking in ankle-high water, is when you decide to walk in faith. Then comes the prayer phase, with its new challenges and some struggles in the quest to live differently. At this level, it is as if the water is at knee level. In the next phase, the water hits your waist. This is the level of service at which point you should be ready to carry the burdens of the gospel and to help others. Then comes the final phase, in which you are totally immersed in the Spirit. The level of submission that cures, transforms, and liberates is when a person is entirely in the water, when you jump in headfirst and have to swim in a river that is too deep to cross on foot.

If you are willing to surrender your life to the service of God, then gradually step into the water with Him and dive deeper into faith until your last strand of hair is submerged.

Spiritual awakening begins with inspiration coming from without. Then, once you are already on the road, the real work begins. Keep at it and inspiration will come from within.

REBBE NACHMAN OF BRESLOV

PART 5

Laws
concerning
Miracles

TWENTY-ONE

The Law of Divine Intervention

The eyes of the LORD range throughout the earth to strengthen those whose hearts are fully committed to Him.

2 Chronicles 16:9

When we consider the role of God in our lives—a subject that gains even greater relevance when we become His partners—we cannot disregard the subject of miracles. Miracles, strictly speaking, are extraordinary events that generally cannot be explained. This is why they generate so much controversy.

Of course, you don't have to believe in miracles in order to benefit from the wisdom of the Bible. The twenty-five biblical laws of success presented in our previous book will make a difference in your personal and professional life. Even the concepts addressed in this book, although they go a step further and assume that you have <u>faith</u> in God, do not require you to enter the field of miracles and the supernatural. For example, someone who adopts the practices presented in the Laws of Maximum Quality, Helping Others, and Integrity will experience superior results at work, in their relationships, and in their daily lives.

Nevertheless, you can choose to dive deeper into the waters of <u>faith</u>. Those who are open to this can experience the power of miracles in <u>all</u> areas of life, including their careers and businesses. The Bible shows that God works miracles in any setting.

Those who are more skeptical, however, may question the possibility of miracles. Are miracles opposed to the laws of nature, as many contend? We don't think so. We think miracles are events that follow laws we still don't understand. ✳
Until the beginning of the twentieth century, science had not discovered the laws that govern the subatomic world. There was only classical Newtonian physics, which correctly explains various phenomena. With the discovery of quantum physics, we were surprised to perceive that there are other laws in this dimension, different from those that govern the visible world. There is no contradiction between classical mechanics and quantum mechanics. They are just different ✓ laws that function and apply to their respective domains.

Likewise, broadly speaking, we could say that miracles are applications of laws we have not yet discovered—just as there was a <u>time</u> when we weren't informed about the subatomic universe and, even so, it kept on working. Now that we have begun to understand the laws that govern the subatomic world, we can do things in areas we hadn't previously mastered. Understanding faith better is analogous to opening new doors, as when Michael Faraday, Albert Einstein, Max Planck, Werner Heisenberg, Erwin Schrödinger, Niels Bohr, and others unveiled the world in which the laws of quantum physics rule.

Ultimately, whatever the explanation, a miraculous intervention is the fruit of a spiritual reality superior to any law of physics, and it is something that can be experienced by anyone through faith.

The good news is that even though no one has been able to establish a formula for faith, we can still put it into practice. If God were a scientist, He would write down mathematical formulas that explain how the sea opens, how bread and fish multiply to feed a multitude, and how a barren woman becomes pregnant. Faith, however, does not operate with formulas. Even so, diseases are cured, lives are changed, and companies and careers are saved. This book doesn't present any mathematical formulas for faith, but it does set forth its practical application. The idea of a partnership with God cannot be reduced to legal clauses in a contract with notarized signatures. Nevertheless, don't doubt that this partnership works.

Miracles can be divine actions, our own actions, or the result of a combination of our acts with those of our partner, God. Regardless of the term you choose to describe them, we hope you get to experience miracles in your life.

God will intervene in your life. Part of this intervention is in the natural realm, and another part is optional. Even when people don't <u>believe</u> in God or follow His principles, ✓ they are still subject to the laws of nature. So whether it is through the laws of physics or the spiritual laws, there will be some divine action in <u>all</u> our lives. Some people, however, want more than this. And for those who seek Him, God intervenes in special ways.

Forms of Divine Intervention

There are <u>two</u> basic forms of divine intervention: through *providence* and through *concurrence*. In the <u>first</u>, God acts alone, providing what we need; in the <u>second</u>, human beings also participate. In addition, there are the following modes of action.

Everyday Miracles

Everyday miracles, or generic miracles, take place when God acts through the natural laws He created that keep the world functioning and people alive.

- "He causes His sun to rise on the evil and the good, and sends rain on the righteous and the unrighteous" (Matt. 5:45 NASB).
- "From your lofty abode You water the mountains; the earth is satisfied with the fruit of Your work. You cause the grass to grow for the cattle, and plants for

people to use, to bring forth food from the earth"
(Ps. 104:13–14 NRSV).

Instructional Miracles

God teaches us the laws of life through the Bible. His instructional miracles are an ordinary method of intervention, for the Bible is available to everyone, but only those who seek its wisdom will benefit.

- "Oh, how I love your law! It is my meditation all day long. Your commandment makes me wiser than my enemies, for it is always with me. I have more understanding than all my teachers, for your decrees are my meditation" (Ps. 119:97–99 NRSV).
- "Be strong and very courageous. Be careful to obey all the instructions Moses gave you. . . . Only then will you prosper and succeed in all you do" (Josh. 1:7–8 NLT).

Supernatural Miracles

Supernatural miracles are the exceptional ways God intervenes in our world. They happen when God alters the natural course of events in order to fulfill His purposes or in response to the prayers of His servants. It is a matter of debate whether supernatural intervention respects the laws of nature (physics, chemistry, biology, etc.). Our position is that these laws continue working perfectly, as we discussed earlier. Even though several studies attest to the power of faith, we still know very little about it.

- "He rescues and He saves; He performs signs and wonders in the heavens and on the earth" (Dan. 6:27).
- "He does great things too marvelous to understand. He performs countless miracles" (Job 5:9 NLT).

Individualized Miracles

Individualized miracles occur when God, for some reason, acts specifically for an individual or group of individuals. This intervention may relate to what the person does (prayer or merit), or it may simply be the will of God. One example is when God, in His sovereignty, chose Israel as His people. Another example is that though there were many shepherds in Israel, David was the one God chose to be king. But this choice doesn't seem arbitrary; it was at least partly due to the way that David acted and thought, demonstrating faith and courage.

God's individualized miracles reveal His nature and His personal care toward human beings, and they can be *selective* or *merciful*. In the case of selective miracles, God's acts are related to some merit or human action. The story of David applies here, because his faith and courage contributed to his being selected by God. Consider other examples of individualized miracles:

- *God chose the Levites to carry the ark of the covenant.* "No one but the Levites may carry the ark of God, because the LORD chose them to carry the ark of the LORD and to minister before Him forever" (1 Chron. 15:2).

- *God honored King Uzziah with protection and help.* "He sought God in the days of Zechariah, . . . and as long as he sought the LORD, God made him prosper" (2 Chron. 26:5 NKJV).

- *God blessed Hagar's descendants.* "[The angel of the LORD] added, 'I will give you more descendants than you can count.' The angel also said, 'You are now pregnant and will give birth to a son. You are to name him Ishmael (which means "God hears"), for the LORD has heard your cry of distress'" (Gen. 16:10–11 NLT).

- *God treats us better than we deserve.* "He has not dealt with us according to our sins, nor rewarded us according to our iniquities" (Ps. 103:10 NASB).

Concurrent Miracles

Concurrent miracles occur when God makes use of the actions of men and women to achieve some purpose. It is at this point that our partnership with God comes to the forefront. This concurrent, or simultaneous, action can happen in a way that is traditional (when both parties act), isolated (when God acts alone, after some prayer), or mitigated (when the person does take action, but the act itself is not enough ✓ to produce the desired result).

As examples of these miracles, we can cite the multiplication of oil and flour recorded in 1 Kings 17. There was a terrible period of drought in the area, and Elijah was thirsty and hungry. He asked a widow in Zarephath to bring him water and bread. She replied that she had only enough oil and flour to make a final meal for herself and her child, and after eating it they would die. Elijah told her to do as she had said but to make bread for him first. He assured her that the flour and oil would not run out until the Lord sent rain. The woman did her part, attending to the request of Elijah, and God did his, multiplying the widow's oil and flour.

We can also cite the resurrection of Lazarus in John 11. Jesus commanded them to remove the stone. Martha, Lazarus's sister, said that as it had already been four days, it would smell bad. Jesus answered, "Did I not tell you that if you believe, you will see the glory of God?" (v. 40). They moved the stone out of the way, and Jesus raised Lazarus.

Another important example is that of the widow in 2 Kings 4. After she lost her husband, the creditors came and wanted to take her two sons to be their servants. The woman took her trouble to the prophet Elisha, who asked her, "Tell me, what do you have in your house?" She replied, "Your servant has nothing . . . except a small jar of olive oil" (v. 2).

Elisha then gave a clear command: "Go around and ask all your neighbors for empty jars. Don't ask for just a few. Then go inside and shut the door behind you and your sons. Pour oil into all the jars, and as each is filled, put it to one side" (vv. 3–4). The woman fulfilled what Elisha said, and all the jars she had gathered in the neighborhood were filled. The oil stopped flowing only after the last jar was filled. If she could have collected more jars, she would have had more oil; if fewer jars, there would have been less oil.

In this case we can see ~~that~~ the miracle is proportional to the effort of the believer. God acts miraculously but according to the effort, disposition, and productivity of the person. One might say ~~that~~ in all three examples, the part of people was much easier. But it is always so; God does the part that is impossible for us.

What about Luck?

We discussed luck in *The 25 Biblical Laws of Success*, but here we want to take it a step further. There are a few biblical texts that talk about luck and chance, for example: "Flipping a coin can end arguments; it settles disputes between powerful opponents" (Prov. 18:18 NLT) and "I saw that under the sun the race is not to the swift, nor the battle to the strong, nor bread to the wise, nor riches to the intelligent, nor favor to those with knowledge, but time and chance happen to them all" (Eccles. 9:11 ESV).

When luck or chance touches us, we have a manifestation of generic laws and a strong principle of equality. When God changes our luck and intervenes in an isolated, selective, or merciful manner, we see how the divine laws are applied to those who ask for help. At this point, luck is no longer random but becomes a favorable instrument for those who seek success.

There is no injustice in this because God's favor is available to all. As they say in the legal world, "Equity aids the vigilant, not those who slumber on their rights." In other words, if you have a right but don't pursue or defend it, you can't complain later. This is the case here: God is available to help, but He respects the personal decisions of those who do not want His intervention.

God's Sovereignty

We must not forget that God governs all. Only God, in His sovereignty, can determine when and how He will act. This may make us uncomfortable and perhaps confused, but only God can determine when there will be exceptions to how things must be. Sometimes when we think He isn't doing anything, it feels as if we are experiencing the silence of God. Those who do not believe in the Creator also deal with mystery, calling it "destiny," "chance," "luck," or "misfortune."

This book is based on the assumption that God intervenes in the right measure. After all, a perfect God would not intervene in the wrong measure. The problem is that we, in our imperfection, sometimes fear that God won't know how to act. Fortunately, He will act in just the right way because He is a good, wise, and powerful Father. And once you get to know and understand how God acts, you will be able to better deal with the spiritual dimension of your life.

God is more interested in having a partnership with you than He is in performing miracles. Miracles are not the heart of a relationship with God. The heart of the relationship is intimacy with Him and redemption through the Messiah. These mark the beginning of a partnership that will affect all areas of your life: marriage, family, work, emotions, finances, and so on.

The partnership can be compared to rowing a boat. Imagine you are using one oar and God is using the other. Both of you are rowing in rhythm toward the same destination. Or, if you prefer, picture train tracks. One side is what God has done, divine tracks; the other side is your part, human tracks. As the train passes over both tracks, it moves ahead.

There are two ways to live your life. One is as though nothing is a miracle. The other is as though everything is.

ALBERT EINSTEIN

TWENTY-TWO

The Law of
Human Miracles

Since the beginning of the world men have not
heard nor perceived by the ear, nor has the eye
seen any God besides You, who acts for the one
who waits for Him.

Isaiah 64:4 NKJV

Nick Vujicic, an internationally renowned speaker who was
born without arms and legs, affirms in his book *Life without
Limits* that for a long time he asked God for a miracle: that
one day, upon waking up, he would have arms and legs. Then
after a while, without receiving an answer, he concluded
that God intended that *he* would be the miracle: "I found
happiness when I realized that as imperfect as I may be, I
am the perfect Nick Vujicic. I am God's creation, designed

according to His plan for me. That's not to say that there isn't room for improvement. I'm always trying to be better so I can better serve Him and the world!"[1]

Sometimes God does not work a miracle because He wants us to make our own. When we are in a tough situation, there may be three reasons behind it:

1. We are reaping what we sowed, and only after we have planted other seeds and waited for them to blossom will we be able to reap different results.
2. God is preparing us for some mission, as He did with Joseph, Moses, David, and so many others.
3. God has already given us a mission, precisely where the difficulty is found.

In our book *The 25 Biblical Laws of Success*, we say that "from a practical point of view, an atheist who obeys the biblical laws of success will enjoy much more professional respect than a religious person who doesn't obey these laws. The laws of success do not discriminate."[2] Sometimes people think God is punishing them, but that is not the case. Often, they are just reaping what they have sown.

The biblical story of David serves as an example of a situation in which God prepares us for some mission. When King Saul was hunting him down, David took refuge in the cave of Adullam, which was full of other men who were also being hunted. David could have complained about the place, but instead he trained and transformed those men, who had been rejected by society, into an elite squad (1 Sam. 22:1–5).

As for the third scenario, the greater the difficulty, the greater the demonstration of trust that God places in our ability to be a positive influence right where we are. A good example of this was when God allowed Paul and Silas to be taken unjustly to prison, where they were used to save the jailer and his entire family (Acts 16:25–33).

Whenever there is a difficult situation, reflect on whether you yourself may have produced it by means of your thoughts, choices, or acts; whether life (or God) is trying to teach you something; or whether there is something you can do to help the people around you. Keep in mind what we already said in the Law of Training: when God doesn't change the circum- ✳ stances, it's because He wants to change you.

Miracles Done by People

Human beings can perform miracles. And the first one oc- curs when someone takes a step of faith and decides to serve, ← help, and love his neighbor as himself. In this case, *the person becomes the miracle*. The greatest transformation is the one ⟵ that happens inside of you. In biblical language, you take on a "new spirit," substituting a "heart of stone" for a "heart of flesh" (Ezek. 11:19).

The person who makes the change is the one who is most helped. This person will be the first to reap the fruits of this change. At work, for example, this type of miracle hap- pens when a whiny, selfish, incompetent, or lazy professional decides to change their attitude and becomes an example of excellence. Each biblical law this person puts into practice is a miracle that will bear fruit in their own life and among those around them.

The second type of miracle that people perform is to allow God to act through them to *help someone who is in need.* Imagine that you have decided to do good in the midst of hardship and have chosen to act in a generous and noble way. In this situation, in addition to helping yourself, you also help others. You benefit through the sowing or through the reaping (what you do comes back to you) and also by harvesting the psychological and spiritual payoffs of doing good.

Every person who gives someone in need an opportunity, good advice, a scholarship, or a second chance is being a part of God's plan to give every human being life in abundance (John 10:10). Consider the glowing examples of people such as Mother Teresa of Calcutta and Martin Luther King Jr. and how much they did for others.

Often God performs His miracles through men and women who are available to carry out these missions. These are people who, as a consequence of their partnership with God, sacrifice their own interests, time, and wealth to help others. You do not need to be Mother Teresa to be a vehicle of this type of human miracle; it is possible to make a difference exactly where you are now. Simply improve your attitude. Don't overlook your own personal power. Rubens Teixeira, in *How to Succeed When You're Not the Favorite*, says, "In all that you do give your best, even when they appear to be insignificant things, because that way the opportunity to administer bigger things will soon be given to you."[3] We see this in Jesus's words in Luke 16:10: "Whoever can be trusted with very little can also be trusted with much, and whoever is dishonest with very little will also be dishonest with much."

Miracles Done by God

When God *acts directly*, performing something out of the ordinary, we experience what is traditionally considered a miracle. It is the very moment, for example, in which God stops the sun (Josh. 10:12), parts the Red Sea (Exod. 14:21), or makes the ax head float (2 Kings 6:6). It is when Jesus cures sick people or resurrects them (Mark 5:22–43). In His sovereignty and in the measure that He considers appropriate, God is the one who performs or doesn't perform these special interventions, simply because He is God.

Even if you have never had experiences like these, you need to realize that they do happen. If you don't believe it, that's okay. But at least be open to miracles in which the protagonist is *you*. David conquered Goliath, and you can conquer giants too. Jesus multiplied the bread and the fish to feed the multitude, and you can feed your neighbors. Jesus transformed water into wine to save a wedding reception, and *if you so desire*, He can transform your life as well. When someone changes their life, isn't it like water turning into wine? When a person overcomes a major challenge, isn't it like opening a path in a sea of difficulties?

For skeptics or unbelievers, we can offer irrefutable scientific data that demonstrates that life itself is a miracle. In a recent study, based on NASA's data, astronomers calculated that in the Milky Way alone there are 8.8 billion Earth-size planets that rotate around stars similar to the sun.[4] These planets are found to be habitable in terms of temperature (not too cold, not too hot). And this estimate refers to our galaxy alone! There are billions of other galaxies in the universe, which—from a scientific viewpoint—further increases the probability that there is life on other planets. Yet, up until the moment of this writing, no evidence of life on other planets has been found.

You have to choose between one of two things: either God doesn't exist, and we are really lucky to end up on this planet, or God does exist, and He is betting it all on us. Either way, whichever hypothesis you choose, you need a lot of faith—whether it is in God or in luck! We are among those who believe that the Creator of the universe actually wants to have a partnership with human beings. Every single person—and the planet as a whole—is part of one great divine endeavor.

We don't just believe in miracles; we depend on them. And most of the time, if we become God's partners, we are invited to become a miracle—which, inevitably, will end up producing others.

Miracles are not contrary to nature, but only
contrary to what we know about nature.
AUGUSTINE OF HIPPO

TWENTY-THREE

The Law of Induced Miracles

[Jacob] said, "I will not let you go unless you bless me."

Genesis 32:26 NASB

How can you receive a miracle? Even though it may seem presumptuous to wish for this, there are multiple reports in the Bible and in history of people asking for miracles and getting them. Thus, the evidence shows that God is willing to perform miracles in response to certain circumstances, and the most obvious circumstance is prayer. But praying isn't the only thing you can do to bring about a miracle.

Miracles often occur for those who ask for or seek God's help. There were many blind people in Palestine, but Jesus usually cured only those who asked for it. Even when a blind man sought him out, Jesus asked him what he wanted, though it was obvious his desire was to have his vision restored (Mark 10:51). In other words, when there is a merciful action, it frequently happens in response to those who ask for it.

God's help can be directed at a group of people or one individual. Reading the Bible, we see battles in which God clearly positioned Himself in favor of one of the sides, giving them the victory. The reasons that cause Him to choose one side or another are not always revealed and remain a mystery. God is sovereign in His decisions. Hence, the best advice is to submit to His will. As the Bible says in Deuteronomy 29:29: "The secret things belong to the LORD our God, but the things revealed belong to us and to our children forever, that we may follow all the words of this law." To paraphrase the writer, we could say, "Don't worry about understanding; miracles and faith surpass our understanding."

Again, God is not obligated to perform miracles just because we want Him to. God is not our employee or servant but quite the opposite. Yet it is common for God to perform a miracle when someone asks Him to, seeks Him, or works for Him. or with Him.

Without losing sight of the fact that wealth and success are not God's priorities, you can certainly ask for His special intervention in your professional life. We can honestly say that we have experienced many victories in our careers because we followed the Bible and the spiritual laws of success. Other times, however, what changed our lives was clearly and undeniably a miracle. People who are more intelligent and more capable than we are have not achieved the things we have achieved. We have made it this far because God has blessed us.

Selective Divine Intervention

God helps everyone, but sometimes His actions are individualized. Selective divine intervention typically occurs for those who are working, those who ask for help, those who dedicate themselves to helping others and to God's service, and those who obey His Word.

God Looks for His Servants While They Are Working

God rarely looks for lazy people. He usually shows Himself to people when they are working. Let's look at some examples:

- Moses was watching his father-in-law's flock when God appeared to him in the burning bush (Exod. 3:1–3).
- Elisha was plowing the field with twelve teams of oxen when he was called to serve alongside Elijah the prophet (1 Kings 19:19–21).
- David was tending his father's sheep when Samuel sent for him (1 Sam. 16:11).
- Simon Peter and his friends were washing the fishing nets when Jesus came to them (Luke 5:1–11).

A curious fact is that when he was called by Jesus to be a fisher of men, Peter didn't leave his boat adrift; instead, he took it ashore, thereby demonstrating that it is important to finish one phase before moving on to the next. In other words, whenever you leave a job, do it in a dignified way, leaving all the doors open. Don't despise or offend anyone at the place you are leaving behind.

Regarding the miraculous fishing episode, Jesus chose men who were dedicated to hard work. If you want God to look for you, then get to work. He will do His part by appearing in the bush and anointing you.

Even though it has been used in another context, Exodus 34:20 can also be applied here: "No one is to appear before me empty-handed." One way to avoid showing up empty-handed before God is to keep your hands busy with some trade or activity.

God Looks for Those Who Seek His Help

The second circumstance that attracts God's attention is prayer or asking for help. In Luke 4:27, Jesus points out, "There were many in Israel with leprosy in the time of Elisha the prophet, yet not one of them was cleansed—only Naaman the Syrian." In what way was Naaman different from others? He looked for the cure, looked for the prophet, and then had the humility to obey the recommendation to bathe in the Jordan seven times.

This is the main path to a miracle: the search, the request, humility, and obedience. The strength of the sum of the first two items, work and prayer, can be summarized in a quote often attributed to Ignatius: "Pray as if everything depended upon God and work as if everything depended upon you."

God Looks for Those Who Help Others

The third force by which someone usually attains God's blessing is serving others. A good example of this is Job, who prayed for his friends who were going to be punished by God and, as a result, was blessed: "After Job had prayed for his friends, the LORD restored his fortunes and gave him twice as much as he had before" (Job 42:10).

When someone is concerned about others, it appears that God becomes concerned with taking care of that person. We will not discuss whether this is a form of compensation or reward or simply the application of spiritual laws. This is not a theoretical book; it is a practical one—and, in practice, when people take care of the children of God, God Himself takes care of them.

God Looks for Those Who Obey His Word

The fourth way in which someone usually receives God's blessing is by exemplary behavior. The more we obey God's Word, the more we are able to receive God's supernatural power in our lives. Along these lines, look at what Jesus says: "If anyone loves Me, he will keep My word; and My Father will love him, and We will come to him and make Our abode with him" (John 14:23 NASB).

However, a person should be careful not to be too focused on obedience (something good) to the point of becoming legalistic (something not good). We should never lose sight of God's loving nature, which is as strong as His just nature. And, of course, we should never forget that He came to grant us grace and unfailing goodwill.

Can God make someone obey Him? Of course, He can. But what we see in the Bible is that God does not usually do the work that should be done by people. Generally, God uses those who are obedient, faithful, and prepared, such as David, Daniel, Paul, and others. God always multiplies what we are, not just what we have. The great sign of His presence in someone's life is not a change in professional or financial situation; it is a change of heart, attitudes, and behaviors. We have heard it said that God loves people so much that He accepts them as they are, and He loves them so much that He will not let them stay that way.

Consistent and Constant Action

Often, we limit the influence and power of a reconnection with God to the context of the church. Yet intimacy with God and a life of spirituality cannot be restricted to just one day a week during a church service. The more you walk alongside Him, the more God will act in your life. Modern society is more attuned to individualism, and human relationships are more and more transitory and utilitarian. Many people desire to relate to God in the same way, as though He were merely someone who answers our prayers, performs miracles, opens doors, and gives us comfort. They are not willing to delve deeper into the relationship because

this requires sacrifice and the readiness to serve your neigh- ✓
bor, to be <u>honest</u>, to show goodwill, and so on. Reflect on
this, and pursue higher standards for your life.

Realize ~~that~~ you are capable of practicing good deeds,
changing your behavior, abandoning addictions, and devel-
oping a generous heart. If you <u>believe</u> you will not find the
strength to do <u>all</u> this alone, rest assured ~~that~~ you can count ✓
on God's help.

---

*I'm not where I need to be, but thank God I'm not
where I used to be. I'm okay, and I'm on my way!*

JOYCE MEYER

TWENTY-FOUR

The Law of Partnership

We are co-workers in God's service.

1 Corinthians 3:9

In the business world, there are specialists called "headhunters" who recruit talented people for large companies. Headhunters search the market for the most qualified professional for a job that needs to be filled. God acts as a "heart hunter." He looks for those who are willing to <u>trust</u> Him and give their hearts to Him, those who are willing to get rid of a "heart of stone" and receive in its place "a new heart" (Ezek. 36:26). This is a miracle born out of partnership. When we are willing to be molded by God, God acts in our lives, giving us a strength we would not have on our own. God proposes to train and support us, but this doesn't mean we are exempt from seeking excellence, overcoming our weaknesses, and dedicating ourselves to our jobs and our studies.

Together, divine and human action will lead us to a condition of stability, peace, and tranquility, which we call prosperity. This is not a gratuitous prosperity, which is limited to material assets, but a condition of holistic well-being, involving health, family, leisure, and service to God and others.

Success results in part from personal effort and in equal measure from God's blessings. The more effort we put in, the more we open the doors to success and divine intervention. God can alone perform miracles, but in general He works with what His partners have in their hands—and He can intervene in all areas of our lives, including our professional and financial lives. It is up to us to decide if we are going to open all the doors for Him or just a few.

God Doesn't Sell Favors

As bold as it may seem, the idea of having a partnership with God is biblical. God is the God of covenants. And throughout the Bible, we see that He has a great deal of goodwill to accept proposals for partnerships, though not all of them are advantageous to Him. Jabez, for example, asked God to change his life, but he didn't offer God anything in return. Amazingly, God heard his proposal and responded to it: "Jabez cried out to the God of Israel, 'Oh, that You would bless me and enlarge my territory! Let Your hand be with me, and keep me from harm so that I will be free from pain.' And God granted his request" (1 Chron. 4:10).

Jacob also asked God for help, but he offered to give a percentage of everything he earned and to build him a temple. This proposal was much better than that of Jabez, but even so, God's "share" in the profits was only 10 percent. We read in Genesis 28: "Then Jacob made a vow, saying, 'If God will be with me and will keep me on this journey ~~that~~ I take, and will give me food to eat and garments to wear, and I return to my father's house in safety, then the LORD will be my God. This stone, which I have set up as a pillar, will be God's house, and of all that You give me I will surely give a tenth to You'" (vv. 20–22 NASB). And God accepted it.

It is important to stress the difference between being generous out of gratitude and trying to buy God's favor. Jacob wanted a real partnership with God and offered his tithe as a form of gratitude. However, later in the Bible, we see ~~that~~ Simon, the sorcerer, sought to receive divine blessings in exchange for money, and his proposal was refused. God doesn't act like that. He wants partners with integrity. This is why Peter censured Simon, the sorcerer: "May your silver perish with you, because you thought you could obtain the gift of God with money! You have neither part nor lot in this matter, for your heart is not right before God. Repent, therefore, of this wickedness of yours, and pray to the Lord that, if possible, the intent of your heart may be forgiven you" (Acts 8:20–22 ESV).

God accepts some proposals without a counterpart and others with assorted percentages. To establish a partnership, God is not very demanding; He accepts all types of people. The Bible features the stories of people who didn't offer anything or very little, but it also speaks of those who dared to give their entire lives—all their belongings and their talents—to God. This was the case of the tax collector Matthew, who gave up a well-paying government position to follow Jesus (Luke 5:27–28). In other words, there are people who surrender 100 percent not only of what they earn but also of who they are to God.

In His relationship with His partners in the Bible, even as He was being loving and gentle, God also demonstrated ~~that~~ He wants those who are in partnership with Him to continue growing and perfecting themselves. Thus, don't be afraid to start a partnership; don't worry if the initial percentage you have to offer God is small. As your partnership progresses, you will be able to make new agreements.

On the Front

As partners, usually God shares tasks with us through divine intervention. Sometimes, however, divine intervention is isolated; in other words, God wins some of our life battles ✓ for us. But when He acts alone, without our participation, He does so based on a previously established partnership. ✓ In these cases, human interaction generally boils down to ✗ prayer and surrendering the matter to God.

We have an example of isolated intervention when the king of Assyria was on the verge of invading the Holy Land. God reassured Hezekiah, king of Judah, with the following words: "He will not come to this city or shoot an arrow there; and he will not come before it with a shield or throw up a siege ramp against it" (2 Kings 19:32 NASB). The Lord's answer came after Hezekiah asked for his help against the powerful army of the cruel and arrogant Sennacherib, king of Assyria, who was hoping for Hezekiah's surrender. In a single night, an angel killed 185,000 Assyrian soldiers (v. 35), thus protecting the city and giving Hezekiah the victory.

Then there are times when the best thing to do is wait patiently and have faith in God. A number of verses in the Bible refer to these situations, such as: "Rest in the LORD and wait patiently for Him" (Ps. 37:7 NASB) and "I waited patiently for the LORD to help me, and He turned to me and heard my cry" (Ps. 40:1 NLT).

There is also another type of intervention, the mitigated one, in which a person, in faith, attempts something on their own and in their own way but doesn't achieve the expected outcome. In this case, the human action was attempted out of faith. And faith pleases God.

Judges 7:1–8 relates the story of a battle in which three hundred men defeated enemy armies of various peoples. Gideon intended to go into battle with an army of thirty-two thousand men. Ultimately, God allowed him to go with only three hundred soldiers; he didn't want the men to think they had achieved victory by their own strength when it was God Himself who won the battle.

Deepening Your Partnership with God

A partnership with God should go above and beyond your career, company, and business. It means becoming God's partner in the great adventure of life. Applying these twenty-five biblical laws of partnership with God only to achieve professional success may work, but it would be sad to see someone perform good actions simply to get rich. Focusing on faithfulness to God is better. In this event, the results will still come, maybe even on a larger scale, and the impact will affect other areas of your life and bring harmony to your family.

Christianity begins with forgiveness, redemption, and salvation, but then it proposes a change of heart and behavior that is not as easy as being saved by faith. Salvation is easy; sanctification—growing in Christlikeness—is not. Everyone wants to receive miracles, but there is a cost to partnering with God. Jesus said that He would give rest to the weary and oppressed and that His yoke is easy and His burden is light (Matt. 11:28–30). But note: there is a *yoke*, and there is a *burden*. This book asks you to reflect on Jesus's yoke and burden in all your surroundings.

As God's partner, you will be challenged to take biblical values to the everyday lives of people and companies. Partners who talk about God but still cheat and steal; reap excessive profits; mistreat employees, clients, children, and spouses; and do not show love and solidarity are anything but good servants. The right thing to do is to repent and change—and bless others with good deeds.

The prophet Isaiah (58:6–11) revealed that a healthy devotion to God is expressed more through acts of justice and goodness than by fasting and religious celebrations. Fasting and prayer please God less than repentance, loving your neighbors, and practicing justice.

The Bible proposes an alternative model for the planet and its people. First Peter 2:15 says, "For it is God's will that by doing good you should silence the ignorant talk of foolish people." On the one hand, when people practice what the Bible teaches, sooner or later they will be recognized as those who always do their best. Everyone around them will note the difference: their boss, subordinates, colleagues and competitors, and family and friends. Their actions will bring benefits and excellent results, as much for them as for the promotion of the Word of God. On the other hand, when people say they follow biblical principles but they lack character, their actions will create the opposite effect and push people away from God.

The Bible says, "Let us throw off everything that hinders and the sin that so easily entangles. And let us run with perseverance the race marked out for us" (Heb. 12:1). We should walk in righteousness, have perseverance, and focus on our objective. Working well is also a form of preaching. Paul says that Christians are "a letter from Christ" that will be known and read by all (2 Cor. 3:2–3). Our lives, when they match our words, can greatly impact others. A partnership with God involves not only having faith but also doing good.

The only thing necessary for the triumph
of evil is for good men to do nothing.
EDMUND BURKE

TWENTY-FIVE

The Law of Eternal Success

Examine everything carefully; hold fast to that
which is good.

1 Thessalonians 5:21 NASB

In James 4:13 we read, "Listen, you who say, 'Today or tomorrow we will go to this or that city, spend a year there,
carry on business and make money.'" This verse is often used
in reference to undertaking something new, but the original
meaning of this passage, as we see in verse 14, is to alert us
~~that~~ our plans should take into consideration the instabil-
ity of life: "Why, you do not even know what will happen
tomorrow. What is your life? You are a mist that appears
for a little while and then vanishes." Because the mist will
soon disappear, Jesus warns us, "What good will it be for

186

someone to gain the whole world, yet forfeit their soul? Or what can anyone give in exchange for their soul?" (Matt. 16:26). This question, which is repeated in Mark 8:36 and Luke 9:25, begs an answer.

The Law of Eternal Success is the last and the most important of the twenty-five biblical laws of partnership with God. And as is the case with all the others, its application depends on you alone. You are the one who will decide whether to follow it, and you are the one who will have to assume the consequences of your choice. Sowing is optional, but reaping is unavoidable—and you cannot plant one type of seed and hope to reap the fruit of another. This is true of all the laws of nature, including the biblical laws. The Law of Eternal Success is essential because it deals with life after death.

One of the greatest contributions of our books about the biblical laws of success and partnership with God is to show people that the Bible is a book of ancient wisdom that provides valuable lessons for their professional lives. The courageous attitude at this point is to be determined to identify what is right and what is wrong on your career path, to be proactive in order to make the necessary changes, and to keep the principles and the guidelines in mind always.

In *The 25 Biblical Laws of Success*, we presented concepts that can be applied by everyone, regardless of whether they have faith or practice a religion. But here, in *The 25 Biblical Laws of Partnership with God*, there is no way to avoid the question of spirituality. When you are in partnership with

God, there are behaviors that only make sense for those who believe in the God who acts and is both just and good. Even though the focus of our study is professional, financial, and personal success, we cannot lose sight of the fact that the Bible also speaks of life after death.

After all, what use is it for you to enjoy professional and financial success for fifty, seventy, or ninety years but not spend eternity in heaven? Imagine living for one hundred years on earth, surrounded by wealth and plenty, only to end up in hell for eternity. That would be worse than earning a million dollars a month and then, upon retirement, being forced to live on a minimum monthly wage without any access to previous possessions or investments. Selling your soul to the devil in order to have a successful life on earth and failing when it comes time to choosing where you will spend eternity isn't worth it.

Jesus says, "One's life does not consist in the abundance of the things he possesses" (Luke 12:15 NKJV). It consists in living in peace here on earth and ensuring eternal life in the best place possible. In short, it's no use following all the other biblical laws and forgetting about the Law of Eternal Success. This law proposes that, in addition to your professional and financial success, you add the success of your soul, which is everlasting.

Faith often requires high levels of generosity and sacrifice, which aren't often associated with people's visions of success. We are referring to another model of success, lived out by ordinary people who by grace were able to do the extraordinary. The apostle Paul, though he faced many difficulties—imprisoned many times, beaten with rods, stoned, shipwrecked, and subjected to hunger and thirst—did not stop serving God (2 Cor. 11:24–28).

Paul, Jesus, and Martin Luther King Jr. are all examples of success, but none of them were rich or had an easy life. All of them experienced suffering and died for their ideals. This is why we shouldn't have a shortsighted view of success ~~that is~~ limited to popularity and fortune.

Trials serve to strengthen men and women of faith. Through his difficult experiences, Paul was able to claim, "I can do all things through Him who strengthens me" (Phil. 4:13 NASB).

Those who don't put their trust in God cannot count on this extra strength, which is capable of raising spirits and complementing our efforts when we are troubled or at risk. But anyone who has not yet put their faith in Christ can, if they ~~wish~~ desire, embark on this type of spiritual journey.

Arriving Where Faith Leads

An important paradigm for salvation is to understand that reconnection with God and eternal life are not obtained by anything we do but through the sacrifice of Jesus Christ. For those who are accustomed to a system of personal merit and effort, this is difficult to understand. In this case, however, the only personal effort that is necessary is for us to recognize that we are imperfect and in need of the grace of God. Then, receiving Jesus as Lord and Savior, we are justified before the God who is perfect.

The fact that we are saved by God's grace, without deserving it, can be seen throughout the New Testament, as in this passage: "It is by grace you have been saved, through faith—and this is not from yourselves, it is the gift of God" (Eph. 2:8). In Jesus's parable recorded in Matthew 20:1–15, those who worked longer, beginning in the morning, received the same pay as those who were hired at the end of the day. This means that the important thing is not what you deserve but the generosity of the giver. It is not about payment; it's about salvation.

After salvation, we should follow a process of maturing and changing our lives, which the Bible calls sanctification. Forget the stereotypical idea of a saint as something inaccessible. Scripture says that we should be saints ("Be holy, because I am holy" [1 Pet. 1:16]), behaving in a new way. As the Bible says in James 2:26: "As the body without the spirit is dead, so faith without deeds is dead."

The Bible says that in order to have success in life after death, you must recognize Jesus Christ as the Son of God. He was born into the world, completed his ministry, died though innocent in order to pay for our sins, and was resurrected. Jesus promised that we would be with him after death if we followed him (John 14:3). That is why it doesn't make sense for us to use the Bible to live well here on earth but not use it to live well in eternity. Take advantage of the wisdom in this ancient book to grow your business and your career, but don't squander the opportunity to get to know Jesus and the transforming power he can have in your life.

God loves you enough to accept you the way you are, and he loves you enough to want you to become a better person. For those who have given their lives to Jesus and are looking to follow the teachings of the Bible, our advice is not to underestimate how much the Bible can also help you in your professional development. Pay more attention to its guidance when it comes to work, and change the way you do things if necessary.

Let God be a part of your life. He cares about your well-being and success. He works with us. In fact, he works even when we are sleeping, as Ron Mehl explained in his book *God Works the Night Shift*.[1] Many people exhaust their strength in order to improve their lives, but they still won't receive even half of what God has in store for those who follow him and trust in his power. Have hope in the One who left us this promise: "Call to me and I will answer you and tell you great and unsearchable things you do not know" (Jer. 33:3).

Those who believe only in themselves project only what they understand to be plausible in their own eyes. This is normal. But those who believe in the existence of God project what their faith is able to reach—and the power of God is limitless. He "is able to do immeasurably more than all we ask or imagine, according to his power that is at work within us" (Eph. 3:20).

We have already proven this in practice. We never imagined we would arrive where we have. We have a partnership with God although he doesn't need to do anything to have a privileged place in our hearts. He can take us where our minds have not yet arrived. This is true for us and for all who believe in him.

Fulfilling your life mission on earth is an essential part of living for God's glory. The Bible gives several reasons why your mission is so important. Your mission is a continuation of Jesus' mission on earth.

RICK WARREN

PART 6

The Seven Mistakes *That Get in the Way* of Success

TWENTY-SIX

The Mistake of Believing Ambition Is Sinful

> The blessing of the LORD brings wealth, without painful toil for it.
>
> Proverbs 10:22

Mistaken mind-sets about <u>faith</u>, money, and business can lead to stagnation and failure. In our previous book, *The 25 Biblical Laws of Success*, we explained the seven cardinal sins against success for those looking to improve their lives. Here we will explore the seven most common mistakes ~~that~~ people and religious institutions make in the name of God, even when they are done in good <u>faith</u>.

You cannot build a solid house on a crooked foundation. So we need to tear down false concepts, many of which are due to misinterpretations of the Bible.

We shouldn't confuse religion as it relates to reconnecting with God—which is essentially good—with religion as it

relates to an institution. Institutional religion is man-made
and fallible because it faces problems ~~that are~~ inherent to ✓
human nature. Mistakes made by people who act in the name
of God can shock and upset us, but we shouldn't lose sight
of the positive side of religion just because some people do
things we don't agree with. We shouldn't give up the proper
causes just because they happen to be in the wrong hands.

When it comes to work, business, and money, there are
two main lines of thought in the church. On the one hand,
there are those who consider success a sin, and hence they
discourage the desire for growth and the effort to improve
their lives. We call this the "theology of misery." On the other
hand, there are those who embrace "prosperity theology,"
which confuses spiritual life with wealth and sees material
success as a mandate from God and a sign of spiritual ap-
proval. Both lines of thought are wrong; they lack balance
and biblical support.

<u>True</u> prosperity goes way beyond mere financial results
and includes physical health, healthy relationships, credibil- ✓
ity, peace, and happiness.

Another common misconception is to assume ~~that~~ God
alone will work for our success without us even lifting a ✓
finger. The opposite misconception is to think ~~that~~ God is
too big to care about our personal and professional fulfill- ✓
ment. Both concepts are wrong because they do not follow
biblical teaching. Lastly, there are many who blindly cling to
misleading biblical self-help clichés and good luck charms.
As Jesus said, "You will know the <u>truth</u>, and the <u>truth</u> will
set you free" (John 8:32 NLT).

Many people, especially in our home country of Brazil, feel a sense of guilt or contempt toward success, even if it has been obtained through studies, effort, and work. This view can result from the culture or from a person's upbringing or spiritual education.

Some religious people believe you shouldn't seek success, much less ask God for help to attain it, for this would indicate selfishness and greed. Those who think this way believe that the desire to improve their lot in life is distasteful, wealth is tainted, and ambition is a sin. But that isn't so! The Bible condemns *selfish* ambition, not the sort of ambition that seeks a better quality of life for you and your family.

The warning in the Bible is clear: "Don't be selfish; don't try to impress others. Be humble, thinking of others as better than yourselves" (Phil. 2:3 NLT) and "The tongue also is a fire, a world of evil among the parts of the body" (James 3:6). But nowhere is it written in Scripture that it is wrong to desire a good job, to wish to start a business, or to seek professional growth.

This distorted view comes from a misinterpretation of certain biblical passages. For example, Romans 12:16 says, "Do not be proud, but be willing to associate with people of low position." Many believe that living humble lives means not having major goals. Humility doesn't result from our financial situations, but rather from a mind-set. There are simple and humble rich people, and arrogant and haughty poor people. And vice versa.

Many people incorrectly conclude that God condemns success, but they forget that many major figures in the Bible, such as Abraham, Isaac, Jacob, David, Solomon, and others, sought to grow and to reach highly ambitious goals, often in the name of God.

The meaning of Romans 12:16, according to the original Greek, is that one should avoid vanity and pride and instead focus on simple things. This verse is reminiscent of the Law of Contentment, covered in *The 25 Biblical Laws of Success*, which deals with the virtue of being satisfied with what you have. This does not mean we should become complacent, but we do need to know how to give value to what we have achieved without continually seeking more and more.

Achieving success and getting rich are not incompatible with a good life before God. People often comment that the Bible says "money is the root of all evil," but that is not what is written. The problem is the *love* of money: "The love of money is the root of all kinds of evil" (1 Tim. 6:10 NLT). In other words, money should not be the priority in our lives. We should have a healthy relationship with it, without rejection or excessive attachment, so that our money can serve us. &others.

The rejection of prosperity, or even a certain disgust toward it, creates a mental barrier to success. The belief that being rich is shameful generates a lack of interest in growth and professional advancement. We know many Christians who refuse to give much thought to secular life, work, and their financial situation, and hence are unemployed or underemployed, unhappy, frustrated, and in debt—which doesn't make anyone happy, nor does it please God.

Various biblical texts explain that God's desire is for us to have good and happy lives, as this Old Testament passage indicates: "The LORD will guide you continually, giving you water when you are dry and restoring your strength. You will be like a well-watered garden, like an ever-flowing spring. Some of you will rebuild the deserted ruins of your cities. Then you will be known as a rebuilder of walls and a restorer of homes" (Isa. 58:11–12 NLT).

In regard to financial debt, it's not only personal finance manuals that say we should avoid it. The Bible also addresses this issue: "Owe nothing to anyone" (Rom. 13:8 NLT); "The borrower is slave to the lender" (Prov. 22:7); and "You were bought with a price; do not become slaves of men" (1 Cor. 7:23 NASB).

Many religious people think that success, fortune, and power lead individuals away from God. Actually, these things just magnify what you already are. No one loses their faith or good principles because they get rich. Power, money, and wealth don't change people; these things just reveal their true nature more clearly: whether they are generous or selfish, upright or corrupt, good or bad managers. "Whoever can be trusted with very little can also be trusted with much, and whoever is dishonest with very little will also be dishonest with much" (Luke 16:10).

Of course, people can change, but what brings this change about is their consciences, their studies, their life experiences, or divine help—rarely their bank accounts.

The one thing that matters is the effort. It continues,
whereas the end to be attained is but an illusion of
the climber, as he fares on and on from crest to crest;
and once the goal is reached it has no meaning.

ANTOINE DE SAINT-EXUPERY

TWENTY-SEVEN

The Mistake of Overestimating Fame, Power, and Wealth

Command those who are rich in this present world not to be arrogant nor to put their <u>hope</u> in wealth, which is so uncertain, but to put their <u>hope</u> in God, who richly provides us with everything for our enjoyment. Command them to do good, to be rich in good deeds, and to be generous and willing to share. In this way they will lay up treasure for themselves as a firm foundation for the coming age, so ~~that~~ they may take hold of the life that is <u>truly</u> life.

1 Timothy 6:17–19

The opposite of the previous mistake, that ambition is sinful, is <u>believing ~~that~~</u> only rich people are blessed. People who feel this way forget ~~that~~ Jesus's family was poor. Just as you should not reject the idea of growth, you also should not make money your top priority, nor act as though it is God's duty to provide it.

Some people avoid the poor and want to build relationships only with the rich. For them, everything revolves around fame, power, and wealth. Those who love money more than righteousness, ethics, or their neighbors may act dishonestly in order to make greater profits. How many promising careers have been destroyed because an individual—whether it's an executive, a politician, or a maid—for the love of money took what didn't belong to them or engaged in shady deals?

This distorted view of the world generates prejudice and disdain toward those who do menial jobs. And this type of behavior is not well regarded in the business world, where the dominant view is ~~that~~ everyone should be treated equally, with respect toward each role. Interestingly, the Bible recommended this same attitude centuries ago, teaching ~~that~~ all work is dignified and ~~that~~ we should not despise even the humblest jobs. In Paul's first letter to the Corinthians, there is an analogy between the different parts of the body and the functions of men: "In fact, some parts of the body that seem weakest and least important are actually the most necessary. And the parts we regard as less honorable are those we clothe with the greatest care" (1 Cor. 12:22–23 NLT).

God does not desire ~~that~~ His people live in poverty or shame, in need or disgraced. We may sometimes experience these, but they should be temporary. As we said in *The 25*

Biblical Laws of Success: "If you think being rich is bad, you will have problems dedicating yourself to getting ahead in life."[1]

The Bible proposes a life of abundance, fullness, and joy, and not pettiness, poverty, and selfishness. We should abandon the mind-set ~~that~~ scarcity is good so ~~that~~ individuals and society can progress. However, thinking only about money is ✱ one way in which a person can become poor. As the saying goes, "Some people are so poor that all they have is money."

Anyone who ~~wishes~~ desires to partner with God must steer clear of materialism, consumerism, egotism, and individualism. We must take a stand against these by following practices ✓ that lead to success without becoming addicted to success. We must be careful not to fall into temptations, traps, or uncontrolled and damaging desires, which can cause us to fall into ruin and destruction. As Paul writes, "The love of money is a root of <u>all</u> sorts of evil, and some by longing for it have wandered away from the <u>faith</u> and pierced themselves with many griefs. But flee from these things . . . and pursue righteousness, godliness, <u>faith</u>, love, perseverance and gentleness. Fight the good fight of <u>faith</u>" (1 Tim. 6:10–12 NASB).

Gain <u>all</u> you can, save <u>all</u> you can, and give <u>all</u> you can.
JOHN WESLEY

TWENTY-EIGHT

The Mistake of Waiting for God to Do Everything

Be strong.

Joshua 1:6

The old Brazilian adage, "When the corpse finds someone to carry him, he lies back in his coffin and takes a ride," implies that complacency is what keeps people from working toward their own success. Complacent people believe that God will open doors or bless them without them having to lift a finger and get to work.

In part 5, we analyzed a few cases in which God did miracles on His own, but don't assume that this is the rule. When God proceeds in this way, He usually lets us know. If He doesn't, it is because we have to do our part. This is one of the aspects of human responsibility. From the beginning, God gave mankind dominion over things: "God blessed them and said to them, 'Be fruitful and increase in number; fill the earth and subdue it. Rule over the fish in the sea and the birds in the sky and over every living creature that moves on the ground'" (Gen. 1:28). This is what we call a cultural imperative, a divine order to study, acquire knowledge, and grow.

There are numerous biblical passages in which people were commanded to put effort into their endeavors and work hard. Here are some examples:

- *God to Joshua*: "Be strong and courageous, because you will lead these people to inherit the land I swore to their ancestors to give them. . . . Keep this Book of the Law always on your lips; meditate on it day and night, so ~~that~~ you may be careful to do everything written in it. Then you will be prosperous and successful" (Josh. 1:6, 8).
- *David to Solomon*: "Take heed now, for the LORD has chosen you to build a house for the sanctuary; be strong, and do it" (1 Chron. 28:10 RSV).
- *God, through Haggai, to Zerubbabel and Jeshua*: "But now the LORD says: Be strong, Zerubbabel. Be strong, Jeshua son of Jehozadak, the high priest. Be strong, all you people still left in the land. And now get to work, for I am with you, says the LORD of Heaven's Armies" (Hag. 2:4 NLT).
- *Paul to the Ephesians*: "Let the thief no longer steal, but rather let him labor, doing honest work with

his hands, so that he may be able to give to those in ✓
need" (Eph. 4:28 RSV).

- *Paul to the Thessalonians*: "Make it your ambition
  to lead a quiet life: You should mind your own business and work with your hands, just as we told you"
  (1 Thess. 4:11).

If you desire to become God's partner, remember this: both
partners have tasks to carry out. Don't just wait. Don't sur-
mise that it is God's job to bring about your success. He ✓
wants to be your partner, not your employee. It is natural
for you to pray, seek the Bible's teachings, meditate before
making major decisions, and want to hear from God, but
be careful not to become someone who is incapable of good
judgment.

There are people who will not do anything without first
getting some sort of authorization from a religious minister.
They become paralyzed as they wait for signs and prophe-
cies, forgetting that the Bible states these signs "will accompany those who have believed" (Mark 16:17 NASB) and not
the other way around.

Be careful not to make one of these two mistakes: acting
without first getting advice or waiting for an official letter
signed by God before making decisions.

There are others who desire to determine how God should
act, arrogantly giving Him orders, or who see God as an investment opportunity, a financial institution, or a quick fix
for their job and money problems. These people approach

the Creator with various sorts of proposals, for example: "I will give you this, and I want that in return," "God, you have to make me successful," or worse, "I determine ~~that~~ you, God, should make me successful."

These are distorted views of God, as if He were an employee or a supplier rather than the One "who is able to do immeasurably more than all we ask or imagine" (Eph. 3:20). The worst consequence of these attitudes is ~~that~~, by waiting for God to do everything, you don't act and thus miss the chance to achieve great things.

The idea of God as a supplier whom we control may seem more manageable than the idea of a sovereign God, but it isn't. The God-as-supplier perspective is limited to what we ask for and think, whereas the sovereign God has no limits and is capable of helping us achieve success beyond our dreams. God as supplier, if He existed, wouldn't allow any room for a partnership or for personal growth. Supplying people with everything they require is not the way to help them advance in life. Nevertheless, incredible as it may seem, God in His mercy often does help even those who treat Him so shortsightedly.

Take a moment to compare a believer who complacently sits back and waits for God to do all the work to an atheist who diligently works and studies. Which of them is following the good principles taught in the Bible? Who, without even realizing it, is more obedient to divine orientation? Who will reap good fruit and achieve success with their projects?

God is not unjust. He reveals the path to success in the Bible. Any being created by Him, religious or not, will obtain results if they follow His teachings. And those who claim to follow God but refuse to <u>obey</u> His teachings do not have the right to give Him orders like "I want this or that," much less to complain when they are unable to improve their lives.

It is common to see people who act as though their relationship with God, the church, or religion were regulated by a Consumer Defense Code with <u>all</u> sorts of correlated claims and demands. Commonly found among these groups are the "investors," who give much of what they own to advance spiritual causes but treat their donations as a bargaining tool or an investment in divine favors. They don't contribute to the church out of love or sacrifice but with the intention of earning ten, twenty, thirty, or even one hundred times more. They try to establish a sort of commercial relationship with God in which the <u>Creator</u> has the obligation to solve <u>all</u> their problems. God is indeed generous, but He is ✓ not our employee.

This reminds us of a story ~~that~~, sadly, actually happened. A religious woman who lived in a slum area started fasting because she wanted to move to an apartment in a rich neighborhood. She also made her entire family take part in the fasting. This woman died due to her prolonged and foolish fasting. Her relatives, whom she also forced to fast, became sick with serious health issues to the point of being hospitalized.

What exactly did this woman <u>hope</u> to gain by fasting? Most likely, she wanted to get God to make her life better by granting her the comfort and <u>joy</u> of living in a good apartment. Regardless of her sincere spiritual devotion, she did

not really understand biblical teachings. Strictly speaking, a person who claims to believe in God should place Him on a much higher level than money, wealth, or success. You cannot see God in a materialistic light.

We need to rid ourselves of this confusing concept of God, which is inconsistent with the Bible and will not result in the success you desire. How much better would it have been if the woman who died had known and understood biblical passages that countered her expectations, such as "So if we have enough food and clothing, let us be content" (1 Tim. 6:8 NLT) and "Therefore I tell you, do not worry about your life, what you will eat or drink; or about your body, what you will wear. Is not life more than food, and the body more than clothes?" (Matt. 6:25).

What if God had plans for the woman to learn or serve in the very area where she lived? And what if He had planned for her to change her neighborhood through her attitude, example, and entrepreneurship? And what if she and her relatives had continued working and striving—would they not have been able to build a better future?

---

*One of the instinctive characteristics of
the ant—and undoubtedly one of its main
qualities—is its initiative for work.*
WILLIAM DOUGLAS AND DAVI LAGO

TWENTY-NINE

The Mistake of Thinking God Won't Do Anything

Don't be afraid, for I am with you. Don't be discouraged, for I am your God. I will strengthen you and help you. I will hold you up with My victorious right hand.

Isaiah 41:10 NLT

Thinking ~~that~~ God will not act to improve our lives or interpreting His apparent silence as indifference to us is another mistake people make. Some people believe ~~that~~ God isn't concerned about them or ~~that~~ he will not intervene in a specific way in the matters that concern them. Those who believe this about God come up with various explanations to justify why He won't do anything.

There are religious traditions that see God as such a majestic and sublime being that He is not able to care for people on an individual basis. According to this view, God is occupied with the major issues of humanity as a whole and not with the problems of individual people.

Indeed, many religions consider God to be a supreme and distant being. They don't see Him as a deity who has relationships with people. But Christians call God *Father*, which reveals His loving, personal, and relational nature. Throughout the Bible, our Father God introduces Himself, partakes in conversation, and cares about the lives of His children. The only reason for God not to act as a loving Father is due to lack of interest from the person in question. However, when we ask for His intervention, He acts. It might not be how we would like Him to, but God intervenes.

Consider the words of Jesus:

So I say to you: "Ask and it will be given to you; seek and you will find; knock and the door will be opened to you. For everyone who asks receives; the one who seeks finds; and to the one who knocks, the door will be opened. Which of you fathers, if your son asks for a fish, will give him a snake instead? Or if he asks for an egg, will give him a scorpion? If you then, though you are evil, know how to give good gifts to your children, how much more will your Father in heaven give the Holy Spirit to those who ask Him!" (Luke 11:9–13)

Other people believe ~~that~~ God does not care about them because they are sinners or don't deserve it or are not important enough. We believe ~~that~~ Jesus came to die for us precisely *because* we are sinners, so it wouldn't make sense for Him to scorn us for this reason. And to think ~~that~~ we are small or irrelevant indicates ~~that~~ we are erroneously judging God by the same value judgments ~~that~~ society uses. This is definitely not the case.

There are yet others who say they do not want God to do anything for them in the area of career and business. They use arguments such as "God has already given me so much" or "God has more important matters to take care of." It seems they don't understand the idea of an all-powerful, all-knowing, and loving God, and they take on an attitude of pride, as if to say, "Let me try to do it myself" or "I can handle it; I don't need any help."

And, of course, there are those who do not believe in God. The Bible, the source of thousands of years of wisdom, deals with the subject of free will, our right to have or not have faith or religion: "The Lord is the Spirit, and where the Spirit of the Lord is, there is freedom" (2 Cor. 3:17). God does not force anyone to walk in His company. Therefore, those who don't believe in God, and for this reason do not ask God for help, evidently do not allow Him to become a more active partner in their lives, families, careers, and businesses.

What we can conclude from the Word of God is ~~that~~ He knows us down to the smallest detail: "Even the very hairs of your head are all numbered. So don't be afraid" (Matt. 10:30–31). Now, if God watches over such minor things as

211

this, wouldn't He also pay attention to the more important things?

The answer to this question is given in the book of Psalms in which David acknowledges this profound connection with God: "You have searched me, LORD, and You know me. You know when I sit and when I rise; You perceive my thoughts from afar. You discern my going out and my lying down; You are familiar with all my ways. Before a word is on my tongue You, LORD, know it completely. You hem me in behind and before, and You lay Your hand upon me" (Ps. 139:1–5).

Whoever says that God doesn't have time for people fails to take into consideration His omnipotence and omnipresence. Even humans, who are still taking baby steps in technology, can discover where a person is through cell phones and GPS; why, then, wouldn't God be able to track each individual? In today's era of big data and the growth, availability, and exponential use of information, man is capable—by way of systems and networks that he himself created—of knowing what is happening on the other side of the world and of sharing his likes, habits, and friends. Even more so, then, the all-powerful Creator knows who we are, where we are, and what we need.

For these reasons, we recommend that you believe with absolute certainty that God is interested in your life—in every detail of it—and that, in as much as you desire, ask, and allow, He will act in your life. God wants you to do your part, and He will do His: "This is what the LORD says—He who made you, who formed you in the womb, and who will help you: Do not be afraid. . . . For I will pour water on the thirsty land,

and streams on the dry ground; I will pour out My Spirit on your offspring, and My blessing on your descendants" (Isa. 44:2–3). And God never fails.

> *God is our refuge and strength, an*
> *ever-present help in trouble.*
>
> Sons of Korah (Ps. 46:1)

THIRTY

The Mistake of Believing Self-Help Slogans

> I beseech you therefore, brethren, by the mercies
> of God, that you present your bodies a living
> sacrifice, holy, acceptable to God, which is your
> reasonable service.
>
> Romans 12:1 NKJV

As humans, we have an inclination toward the irrational—myths, fables, mysticism, charlatanism, charms, or catch-phrases—as if they contained magic solutions for all our problems. When we talk about being rational, we are not excluding emotion or sentiment, much less spirituality, but rather behavior without any biblical basis. After all, the teachings of this ancient book are the focus of this work.

A mistake that many Christians make is to cite Bible verses as self-help slogans. Worse yet, they often do it out of context! The best example of this is the misuse of the apostle Paul's words, "I can do everything through Christ, who gives me strength" (Phil. 4:13 NLT) as though this verse were an argument for not planning, preparing, or being proactive. We have seen students who have not studied for their university tests and then, right before year-end exams, announced ~~that~~ they were going to pass because "I can <u>do</u> everything through Christ, who gives me strength." And others who said they were going to pay off their debts—accumulated irresponsibly—because "I can <u>do</u> everything through Christ, who gives me strength." To be fair, we must admit ~~that~~ once in a while, God, in His mercy, does provide miraculous solutions for people in need, as we saw in the story of the widow who from her one container of olive oil was able to fill many containers of olive oil, which she sold to pay off her debt (see chapter 21).

Often God gives beyond what we ask for, in spite of our lack of worthiness. We have both experienced this mercy in our lives. That being said, we still need to recognize the mistake in this rationale. Those who use Philippians 4:13 irresponsibly neglect to read the previous verse, in which Paul says, ~~that~~ he is ready to lose or to gain, to have wealth or have nothing, to have plenty or to live in poverty.

Paul was saying ~~that~~ he could do "<u>all</u>" through Christ, who strengthens him, regardless of whether he had material possessions. Paul affirmed ~~that~~ his relationship with God did not depend on how much money or success he had—to the point of even considering the possibility of failure and misfortune.

The Bible clearly states in this passage that in order to win, we need to be prepared to lose—for an occasional defeat will only become definitive if we abandon the war. If we soldier on, we will find a new possibility for success, using our previous experience as a lesson.

The real meaning of the verse "I can do everything through Christ, who gives me strength" is that Paul's relationship with God would not be affected by circumstances. In other words, this is practically the opposite of the distorted, self-help use of the verse.

The expression "God is <u>faithful</u>" is another example of a <u>true</u> statement that is often used out of context. Many people act as if the expression itself has magical powers capable of exonerating mistakes. For example, a person neglects to pay their car insurance and says, "God is <u>faithful!</u>" as if it were up to God to provide protection. It isn't right for someone to neglect to study, work, plan, carry out their duties, or be prudent, and then use this expression as a mantra for protection, a wild card to replace everything they should have done but didn't. The Bible says, "Be shrewd as serpents and innocent as doves" (Matt. 10:16 NASB).

Yes, God is <u>faithful</u>, primarily to what He says—and He said that man would reap what he sows (Gal. 6:7). His advice and orientation are compiled in the Bible so that <u>all</u> can benefit from it. God is <u>faithful</u>. But the question is whether *we* will be <u>faithful</u>, putting into <u>practice</u> what He has <u>taught</u> us.

Some people cite biblical verses indiscriminately, even in business documents. In most cases, these references are used out of <u>faith</u> or gratitude to God, which is good. However, many do not practice what they preach. They fall back on this trick in the hopes of receiving commercial gain—by seeming to be good people and thereby attracting clients and amassing goodwill. This is using faith for spurious purposes. If a person or a company actually runs their business respectably, then all is well. But if they act dishonestly, they bring deep shame to the gospel. It is nothing less than taking the Lord's name in vain (Exod. 20:7).

The ideal path is to dump all these clichés, catchphrases, and babble, and begin to do things according to the Bible.

What you focus on, what you pay attention to,
expands as you move closer to your vision.

WILLIAM DOUGLAS

THIRTY-ONE

The Mistake of Putting More Faith in Superstition Than Action

Why do you call me, "Lord, Lord," and do not *
do what I say?

Luke 6:46

Some religious leaders and Christians condone the use of amulets and trinkets rather than encouraging better attitudes and actions. The use of these objects appeals to the human tendency to want to materialize the spiritual world, as the Israelites did when they built and idolized the golden calf as if it were a god (Exod. 32). It is easier to hold on to objects than it is to change behavior.

Those who follow this path forget the commandment that exhorts us not to make idols (Exod. 20:3–5). And an idol is not just a graven image or statue. It can be any object in which you put your trust instead of God. Whenever you use physical resources to deal with spiritual matters, you engage in idolatry. Even though these behaviors may seem innocent, they are harmful. It doesn't make sense for Christians to use rings, stones, necklaces, paintings, and other such items for protection, luck, or prosperity. For example, anyone has the right to keep in his home a mandala—a diagram composed of geometric forms, utilized by mystics as a source or concentration of energy. But it doesn't make sense for someone who reads the Bible as a guide for faith and behavior to use an object like this, hoping to guarantee protection or help.

There are two situations in which people use such amulets. The first is when a Christian out of naiveté or following fads or in search of a little extra help uses amulets from other religions. Some use the excuse that "it can't hurt" or that "the intention is all that matters," forgetting that this does not please God. The second scenario is when a Christian uses biblical texts, or even tattoos of verses, as if these items possess some type of mystical, spiritual power.

It is one thing to hang a picture with a verse on your wall at home or to leave your Bible open on the table. It is another thing to believe that this, in and of itself, will bring you some form of protection. The One who protects us is the God of the Bible, the God who inspired the verse, and not the Bible or the verse itself. Of course, God is pleased when we have the Holy Scriptures and its teachings displayed in our residence or workplace, showing that we are not embarrassed by our faith. The problem is when you transfer the confidence that only God can give to physical objects—or when you no longer change your behavior or your mind-set because you have gotten used to the false confidence projected by such objects.

Along the same line, another mistake that has become common in religious circles is the exaggerated use of so-called prophetic acts. In the Bible, such acts exist and are inspired directly by God. These are acts that, in and of themselves, would never have any power to produce results without divine intervention. The Bible provides many examples. In Joshua 6, the army of Israel, in order to conquer Jericho, circled the city for six days, and on the seventh day, they circled it seven times. Then the priests blew trumpets, the people shouted, and the walls of the city came tumbling down. In 2 Kings 5, Naaman was cured of leprosy after dipping himself seven times in the Jordan River.

The problem is that it has become a fad to perform prophetic acts like these. We see a multiplication of these kinds of acts, ranging from marches to setting landmarks and including cutting cords, anointing places, and tearing up papers symbolizing this or that. When these are determined by the Spirit of God, they become acts of faith, physical gestures that point to the spiritual realm. But when they are not guided by God, they do not reflect what is in the Bible.

We need balance in all aspects of life, both religious and secular. Acts of faith are valid; in fact, it is worth noting that baptism itself is symbolic. The Bible does allow for some symbols and prophetic acts, but we should avoid the temptation to transform them into a form of idolatry, which is condemned. Most importantly, we should not use these actions as a way to get out of the job at hand—that is, the ways in which we intervene in the real world in partnership with God.

Don't give up when you survive the storm.
You could be close to your goal.

RUBENS TEIXEIRA

THIRTY-TWO

The Mistake of Thinking You Can't Mix <u>Faith</u> and Business

Whoever has my commands and keeps them is the one who loves me. The one who loves me will be loved by my Father, and I too will love them and show myself to them.

John 14:21

Many people <u>believe</u> ~~that~~ <u>faith</u> and business don't go together. They say, ~~that~~ religion is a complicated subject—and when it is misinterpreted, it certainly can be—and shouldn't be placed at the same level as material issues. And there are religious people who seem oblivious to practical everyday matters, such as working, making money, paying bills, and improving life.

One of the greatest mistakes made by those who believe in God is not applying His lessons to all areas of their lives, whether they involve church, home, or work. When we affirm that the wisdom of the Bible can transform careers and businesses, we are not proposing a method just to make a profit and have financial success. We advocate a change that will affect the quality of relationships and the lives of bosses, employees, and clients.

As we have seen throughout this book, mixing religion and business can be extremely beneficial for it brings to the competitive corporate universe a set of fundamental values, such as integrity, excellence at work, and love for our neighbors.

Jesus said, that we should treat others as we would like to be treated (Matt. 7:12). Imagine if bankers, public servants, and service providers were true to this principle. What would happen to excess profits, corruption, and exploiting others? These will no longer occur if a person follows what Jesus commands. Imagine if everyone applied the Golden Rule in business. At the very least, those who claim to be Christians should. Businesspeople, workers, public servants, politicians, and self-employed professionals who carry a Bible, who pray, or who regularly go to church should behave more ethically.

In one case, we have evidence that applying the Golden Rule works. A top executive for the Sony music label told us that in the evangelical CD market, piracy is significantly lower. This is likely due to the awareness that we cannot have something without giving fair remuneration to those who do the work. Imagine what would happen if everyone in this country who presents themselves as Christians would apply the concepts of honesty and integrity in politics, in business, and in paying their taxes.

The other side of this story isn't so pretty. Some Christians are not so upright—for example, business owners and managers who exploit their workers, employees who commit fraud, government officials who ignore ethical standards, and so on. The Bible says, "All who belong to the LORD must turn away from evil" (2 Tim. 2:19 NLT).

If someone claims to be a follower of God but does not act accordingly, he or she is at the same level as those whom Jesus called hypocrites. Consider this biblical passage highlighting the importance of our attitudes:

> What good is it, my brothers and sisters, if someone claims to have faith but has no deeds? . . . Suppose a brother or a sister is without clothes and daily food. If one of you says to them, "Go in peace; keep warm and well fed," but does nothing about their physical needs, what good is it? In the same way, faith by itself, if it is not accompanied by action, is dead. But someone will say, "You have faith; I have deeds." Show me your faith without deeds, and I will show you my faith by my deeds. (James 2:14–18)

It is worth noting that people don't need only food and clothes but also honest and efficient governments, companies that don't exploit their employees or customers, executives who don't sell their souls to the devil in return for astronomical bonuses, workers who aren't dishonest with their bosses, and athletes who don't try to injure their opponents or win by illicit means. Play hard and earnestly, of course! But never unfairly.

Do not make the mistake of separating faith from everyday life by avoiding putting into practice what you say you believe. Instead, choose to follow biblical principles twenty-four hours a day, seven days a week, and not just in church, in public discourse, or when you are being observed by other people.

How refreshing it would be if the political and corporate worlds would listen to this warning: "Woe to him who builds his palace by unrighteousness, his upper rooms by injustice, making his own people work for nothing, not paying them for their labor" (Jer. 22:13). This would affect profits for banks and phone companies, and it would help tackle slave and child labor, tax evasion, labor practices, and pension rights. And what of Jesus's advice to government officials: "Don't extort money and don't accuse people falsely—be content with your pay" (Luke 3:14)?

On the one hand, when the Bible says "woe to him," it is because those who ignore this warning will have to face the consequences of their actions. On the other hand, Scripture indicates that God welcomes those who desire to be redeemed. If a person has already made a mistake, the advice is direct—change: "He who conceals his transgressions will not prosper, but he who confesses and forsakes them will find compassion" (Prov. 28:13 NASB).

If you are someone who has made any of the seven mistakes dealt with in part 6, you can start being someone who puts the Word into practice from now on. Study the Bible seriously and systematically, with faith and zeal, and discover what it really teaches. Examine everything, and retain what is good.

Success will come as a result of study, hard work, and, of course, persistence. If, in a battle, we should lose fifty times and win on the fifty-first time, the fifty losses would simply be what paved the road to a history of perseverance because victory erases the entire history of failure and humiliation.

Be the change you wish to see in the world.
GANDHI

CONCLUSION

Your Opportunity to Live Well

He must turn away from evil and do good; He must seek <u>peace</u> and pursue it.

1 Peter 3:11 NASB

Your life is a gift you have received, and only you can choose what to do with it. God wants you to have a full and abundant life, but it is up to you to make your decisions and choose your path. God will only intervene in a profound way if you allow Him to, if you <u>believe</u> in Him, and if you put His laws into <u>practice</u>. Your willingness to serve God and others will make a difference on your journey.

Incorporating the twenty-five biblical laws of partnership with God into your life is a task that should be undertaken ✓ gradually and without haste. Don't worry if you think you are too far from the ideal; walking in the right direction is more important than your speed or the distance to your goal.

Salvation is a gift, and perfection is a process. This is precisely what is interesting: building a beautiful story and not simply receiving one that is already finished.

In essence, you have the privilege of being alive and being able to choose where you will go, what you will do, and in whose company. This is amazing. Enjoy it. Define your priorities, be calm, and live your life. There is a beautiful verse in the Bible that, though it deals with a specific situation, touches on this point: "Look, the whole country lies before you; go wherever you please" (Jer. 40:4).

Above all, seek to be a success in the eyes of God. You can follow the example of Jesus, who lived to love and serve. He died, was resurrected, and is alive. His revolutionary words endure till this day, two thousand years later. His book, the Bible, is the all-time bestseller. But Jesus also relinquished His comfort and ultimately gave His life for love and for the salvation of many. His inspiring trajectory reaches far beyond a worldview limited to work, business, and material possessions.

You can count on God but do your part. Persevere in order to reap the fruits of the new seeds you have planted. If it takes awhile, don't lose faith. Don't be in a hurry or think that everything happens overnight. Remember that you should enjoy life and the blessings God gives. Knowing how to do this well is an extraordinary gift. More than just thinking about money and a career, living involves seeking success and prosperity in all areas of your life, including health, family, love, leisure, and friendship.

Solomon, a man who looked for fulfillment in all the wrong places, wrote the book of Ecclesiastes after seeking happiness through wealth, work, and power. At the end of his search, he concluded that it was all vanity. Consider the teachings he left us after much reflection:

> Seize life! Eat bread with gusto,
> Drink wine with a robust heart.
> Oh yes—God takes pleasure in your pleasure!
> Dress festively every morning.
> Don't skimp on colors and scarves.
> Relish life with the spouse you love
> Each and every day of your precarious life.
> Each day is God's gift. It's all you get in exchange
> For the hard work of staying alive.
> Make the most of each one!
> Whatever turns up, grab it and do it. And heartily!
> This is your last and only chance at it,
> For there's neither work to do nor thoughts to think
> In the company of the dead, where you're most
>   certainly headed. (Eccles. 9:7–10 MSG)

Don't miss the opportunity to live well. "We need to learn to enjoy the results of our work. The work can and should be rewarding, and we should rejoice with it."[1] So become rich with this rare form of wealth.

I believe in Christianity as I believe that the Sun has risen: not only because I see it, but because by it, I see everything else.

C. S. LEWIS

APPENDIX

The 50 Biblical Laws

THE 25 BIBLICAL LAWS OF SUCCESS
Laws that apply to all people

Laws concerning Wisdom

1. The Law of Opportunity
2. The Law of Wisdom
3. The Law of Vision
4. The Law of Focus
5. The Law of Planning

Laws concerning Work

6. The Law of Work
7. The Law of Courage
8. The Law of Resilience
9. The Law of Joy
10. The Law of Recharging

Laws concerning Values

11. The Law of Self-Hiring
12. The Law of Honesty
13. The Law of Names
14. The Law of the Company You Keep
15. The Law of Self-Control

Laws concerning Relationships

16. The Law of Love
17. The Law of Agreement
18. The Law of Usefulness
19. The Law of Advice
20. The Law of Leadership

Laws concerning Personal Growth

21. The Law of Gratitude
22. The Law of Generosity
23. The Law of Contentment
24. The Law of Employability
25. The Law of Sowing

THE 25 BIBLICAL LAWS OF PARTNERSHIP WITH GOD
Laws associated with faith in God

Laws concerning Faith

1. The Law of Faith
2. The Law of Prayer
3. The Law of Training
4. The Law of Well-Rewarded Affliction
5. The Law of the Garden

Laws concerning Effort

6. The Law of Maximum Quality
7. The Law of the Extra Mile
8. The Law of Entrepreneurship
9. The Law of the Favorable Impression
10. The Law of Loving Leadership

Laws concerning Righteousness

11. The Law of Integrity
12. The Law of the Complete Set
13. The Law of Generous Resiliency
14. The Law of the Ten Steps
15. The Law of Helping Others

Laws concerning Relationship with God

16. The Law of Dependence
17. The Law of Patience
18. The Law of Stewardship
19. The Law of Worship
20. The Law of Submission

Laws concerning Miracles

21. The Law of Divine Intervention
22. The Law of Human Miracles
23. The Law of Induced Miracles
24. The Law of Partnership
25. The Law of Eternal Success

NOTES

Introduction

1. "DEUS EXISTE? Cliente de uma barbearia prova a existência de Deus através de um homem cabeludo. . . !" [Does God exist? A client of a barbershop proves the existence of God through a hairy man], YouTube, July 28, 2017, https://www.youtube.com/watch?v=8CHZVr5MEoY.

Chapter 3 The Law of Training

1. *Something the Lord Made*, directed by Joseph Sargent (HBO Films, 2004).

2. "UFC Rio: Rousimar Palhares," YouTube, August 19, 2011, https://www.youtube.com/watch?v=qXdSuZPj46Q.

3. Niccolò Machiavelli, *The Prince* (São Paulo: Edipro, 2018), chap. 6.

Chapter 4 The Law of Well-Rewarded Affliction

1. Luís de Camões, "Jacob," in *Selected Sonnets: A Bilingual Edition*, trans. William Baer (Chicago: University of Chicago Press, 2008), 147.

2. De Camões, "Jacob," 147.

3. Jim Collins and Jerry I. Porras, *Built to Last: Successful Habits of Visionary Companies* (New York: HarperBusiness, 1994), 202.

4. Baltasar Gracián, *The Art of Worldly Wisdom* (Mineola, NY: Dover Publications, 2005), 19.

Chapter 5 The Law of the Garden

1. Mario Quintana, "Butterflies," Infinite Wisdom, accessed December 30, 2019, http://www.infinitewisdom.it/sito/butterflies/.
2. Philip Kotler, *Marketing 3.0: From Products to Customers to the Human Spirit* (Hoboken, NJ: Wiley, 2010).

Chapter 6 The Law of Maximum Quality

1. Cristiane Correa, *Dream Big* (Rio de Janeiro: Primeira Pessoa, 2014), 46.

Chapter 7 The Law of the Extra Mile

1. Bob Nelson, *Please Don't Just Do What I Tell You, Do What Needs to Be Done: Every Employee's Guide to Making Work More* (Rio de Janeiro: Sextante, 2011), 16.
2. Napoleon Hill, "Lesson Nine," in *The Law of Success in Sixteen Lessons* (Meriden, CT: Ralston University Press, 1928).

Chapter 8 The Law of Entrepreneurship

1. Zack Friedman, "Here are 10 Genius Quotes from Warren Buffett," *Forbes*, October 4, 2018, https://www.forbes.com/sites/zackfriedman/20 18/10/04/warren-buffett-best-quotes/#25ec04614261.

Chapter 10 The Law of Loving Leadership

1. Jorge Gerdau Johannpeter, in discussion with the authors, April 2017.

Chapter 11 The Law of Integrity

1. Lexico, s.v. "integrity," accessed November 22, 2019, https:// en.oxforddictionaries.com/definition/integrity.
2. Erika Andersen, "23 Quotes from Warren Buffett on Life and Generosity," *Forbes*, December 2, 2013, https://www.forbes.com/sites/erika andersen/2013/12/02/23-quotes-from-warren-buffett-on-life-and-gener osity/#75c0ba06f891.
3. Warren Buffett, *The Essays of Warren Buffett: Lessons for Corporate America*, ed. Lawrence Cunningham (Durham, NC: Carolina Academic Press, 2010), 38.
4. Charles H. Spurgeon, "Spurgeon's Maxims for Living," Exploring the Mind and Heart of the Prince of Preachers, accessed November 22, 2019, http://www.spurgeon.us/mind_and_heart/quotes/i.htm.

5. Samuel Johnson, *The History of Rasselas: Prince of Abissinia* (Hertfordshire, UK: Wordsworth, 2000), 76.

6. Warren Buffett, Good Reads, accessed November 22, 2019, https://www.goodreads.com/quotes/577549-honesty-is-a-very-expensive-gift-don-t-expect-it-from.

Chapter 12 The Law of the Complete Set

1. Larry Titus, *The Teleios Man: Your Ultimate Identity* (Oviedo, FL: HigherLife, 2010).

Chapter 14 The Law of the Ten Steps

1. Cecília Meireles, "Mar absoluto" [Absolute sea], in *Antologia Poética* [Poetic anthology] (Rio de Janeiro: Nova Fronteira, 2001).

2. This section includes a summary of the study related in William Douglas, *The Power of the Ten Commandments: The Biblical Path to a Better Life* (São Paulo: Mundo Cristão, 2013), which was inspired by the lessons of Leonard Felder in his work *The Ten Challenges* (Salem, WI: Sheffield Publishing, 2004).

Chapter 15 The Law of Helping Others

1. Rubens Teixeira, *How to Succeed When You're Not the Favorite* (São Paulo: Print International, 2016), 84–85. See also Tami Simon, "Jim Hunter on Servant Leadership," DailyGood, August 7, 2014, http://www.dailygood.org/story/786/jim-hunter-on-servant-leadership/.

2. "Peace Prayer of Saint Francis," Loyola Press, accessed November 26, 2019, https://www.loyolapress.com/our-catholic-faith/prayer/traditional-catholic-prayers/saints-prayers/peace-prayer-of-saint-francis.

Chapter 18 The Law of Stewardship

1. Jack Welch interviewed by Bill Hybels, "Leader to Leader," Global Leadership Summit (Willow Creek Association, 2010), DVD.

2. Kahlil Gibran, "On Children," *The Prophet* (New York: Alfred A. Knopf, 1923), 17–18.

Chapter 19 The Law of Worship

1. *Facing the Giants*, directed by Alex Kendrick (Albany, NY: Sherwood Pictures, 2006).

Chapter 20 The Law of Submission

1. Rick Warren, *The Purpose Driven Life: What on Earth Am I Here For?* (Grand Rapids: Zondervan, 2002), 17.
2. Joyce Meyer, *The Spiritual Man and Discernment* (Fenton, MO: Joyce Meyer Ministries, n.d.), DVD.

Chapter 22 The Law of Human Miracles

1. Nick Vujicic, *Life without Limits* (Colorado Springs: WaterBrook, 2010), 1.
2. William Douglas and Rubens Teixeira, *The 25 Biblical Laws of Success* (Grand Rapids: Baker Books, 2017), 170.
3. Teixeira, *How to Succeed When You're Not the Favorite*, 62.
4. Seth Borenstein, "8.8 Billion Habitable Earth-size Planets Exist in Milky Way Alone," NBC News, November 4, 2013, https://www.nbc news.com/sciencemain/8-8-billion-habitable-earth-size-planets-exist -milky-way-8C11529186.

Chapter 25 The Law of Eternal Success

1. Ron Mehl, *God Works the Night Shift: Acts of Love Your Father Performs Even While You Sleep* (Sisters, OR: Multnomah, 2006).

Chapter 27 The Mistake of Overestimating Fame, Power, and Wealth

1. Douglas and Teixeira, *25 Biblical Laws of Success*, 194.

Conclusion

1. William Douglas and Davi Lago, *Formigas* [Ants] (São Paulo: Mundo Cristão, 2016), 99.

William Douglas is a federal judge in Rio de Janeiro, Brazil, a university professor, a popular speaker, and the author of thirty-five books, including the Brazilian edition of *The 25 Biblical Laws of Success*, with over 250,000 copies sold. He is part of Educafro, a Brazilian organization working to prevent racial prejudice and promote equal opportunities, and is the entrepreneurship coordinator for social projects for United Missions, part of the Brazilian Baptist Convention. He is also part of the Brazilian Evangelical Academy of Writers.

Rubens Teixeira is former CFO of Petrobras Transporte S.A. (Transpetro) and an analyst for Central Bank of Brazil, as well as a professor, writer, and frequent panelist. He was honored with the National Treasure Prize for his PhD thesis with proposals for the Brazilian economy and is the author of *How to Succeed When You Are Not the Favorite* and the coauthor of *The 25 Biblical Laws of Success*. He holds a civil engineering degree and a master's degree in nuclear engineering from the Military Institute of Engineering, a law degree and PhD in economics from the Federal University of Brazil (UFF), and a military science degree from the Military Academy of Agulhas Negras. He is also part of the Brazilian Evangelical Academy of Writers.

Connect with
William & Rubens at

25BiblicalLaws@WilliamDouglas.com.br

f @PaginaWilliamDouglas

𝕏 @Site_WD

▶ SiteWilliamDouglas

◉ SiteWilliamDouglas

WilliamDouglas.com.br

f @Dr.RubensTeixeira

𝕏 @RubensTeixeira

▶ user/AmigosRubensTeixeira

◉ RubensTeixeira_

RubensTeixeira.com.br

Time-tested laws of success that will
TRANSFORM YOUR CAREER

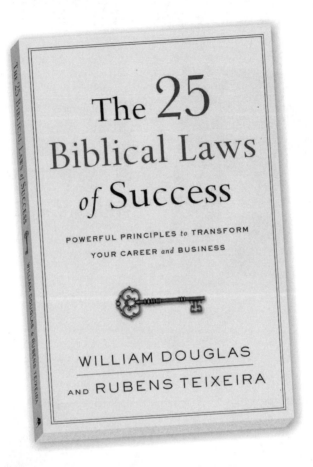

The Bible offers powerful, proven principles that can lead to a life of great success today. After years of biblical study and personal experience, William Douglas and Rubens Teixeira identified twenty-five key principles that are vitally important to the pursuit of success.